D1102425

Th

Ur   ning

13 JUL 2015

− 9 MAR 2019

THE LONDON BOROUGH
www.bromley.gov.uk

ORPINGTON LIBRARY
01689 831551

Please return/renew this item
by the last date shown.
Books may also be renewed by
phone and Internet.

Bromley Libraries

30128 80014 660 0

Also available from Continuum

How to be a Successful Teaching Assistant – Jill Morgan

The Teaching Assistant's Guide to Managing Behaviour – Jill Morgan

101 Essential Lists for Teaching Assistants – Louise Burnham

Complete Guide for Teaching Assistants in Secondary Education – Geoff Brookes

The Teaching Assistant's Handbook: Primary Edition – Janet Kay

The Teaching Assistant's Guide to Literacy – Susan Elkin

The Teaching Assistant's Guide to Numeracy – Sara Fielder

The Teaching Assistant's Guide to ADHD – Kate Spohrer

The Teaching Assistant's Guide to Autistic Spectrum Disorders – Ann Cartwright and Jill Morgan

The Teaching Assistant's Guide to Dyslexia – Gavin Reid and Shannon Green

The Teaching Assistant's Guide to Dyspraxia – Geoff Brookes

The Teaching Assistant's Guide to Emotional and Behavioural Difficulties – Kate Spohrer

The Teaching Assistant's Guide to Understanding and Supporting Learning

Madeleine Graf with Ann Birch

network
continuum

Bromley Public Libraries	
ORP	
30128 80014 660 0	
Askews	25-Feb-2009
371.14124 EDU	£16.99

Continuum International Publishing Group
The Tower Building   80 Maiden Lane, Suite 704
11 York Road   New York, NY 10038
London, SE1 7NX

www.continuumbooks.com

© Madeleine Graf with Ann Birch 2009

All rights reserved. No part of this publication may be reproduced or transmitted in any form or by any means, electronic or mechanical, including photocopying, recording, or any information storage or retrieval system, without prior permission in writing from the publishers.

Madeleine Graf and Ann Birch have asserted their right under the Copyright, Designs and Patents Act, 1988, to be identified as Author of this work.

British Library Cataloguing-in-Publication Data
A catalogue record for this book is available from the British Library.

ISBN: 9780826493682 (paperback)

Library of Congress Cataloguing-in-Publication Data
A catalog record for this book is available from the British Library.

Typeset by YHT Ltd, London
Printed and bound in Great Britain by
CPI Antony Rowe, Chippenham, Wiltshire

Contents

Acknowledgements

With thanks to colleagues working on the Foundation degree in Learning Support at Swansea Metropolitan University and to the TA students who work so hard to support children's learning.

Introduction

There are now several series of books written for TAs, including books on learning. This book adopts a very particular approach as the contents of several of the chapters, and the case studies used as illustrations, are based explicitly on the experiences and contributions of TAs attending CPD (continuing profession development) courses, including a Foundation degree in learning support. This is a deliberate approach intended to recognize and value the experiences of TAs and to show how these experiences can be built upon to extend understanding.

The first chapter introduces three people who have made major contributions to learning theory: Piaget, Vygotsky and Bruner. It then goes on to discuss a theory of learning called social constructivism. You will be able to follow the main principles of this theory as threads that run through the rest of the book. You will also notice that some ideas occur in more than one chapter; this is an indication that with learning it is impossible to put elements into discrete boxes.

The rest of the book tries to bring together theory and classroom practice, and makes reference to curriculum documents and guidelines where appropriate. Documents from both England and Wales have been used. The two education departments: in England, the Department for Children, Schools and Families (DCSF) formerly the DfES, and in Wales, the Department for Children, Education, Lifelong Learning and Skills (DCELLS), publish separate and increasingly different curriculum documents and guidance. The National Curriculum documents are specific to either England or Wales but the guidance and support materials are generally useful wherever you are. A full reference list is included if you want to read more about any of the topics discussed and more resources can be found in the 'Where Can You Go Next?' section at the end of the book. Throughout the chapters you will find invitations to reflect, answer questions and perform short tasks. I hope you will take the time to do what is suggested, as active involvement and reflection are important ingredients of learning for all of us.

Why learn about learning?

As TAs you are at the forefront of supporting the learning of the pupils you work with. Some of you will be involved in actively teaching a class or group but, in the main, the teaching will be carried out by the class teacher and you will be there to support the learning. If you are going to do this well it is important that you have an understanding of how learning happens and of some of the factors that influence and affect learning. This book looks at some factors such as classroom organization, learning styles, and social and emotional aspects of learning, but also discusses and tries to draw the connections between how children learn, according to social constructivist theory, and ways of working in the classroom. This is why time is spent on assessment for learning, learning communities and learning to learn.

Several chapters give you ideas that you can try out with your pupils. If you try something new make sure that you make time to reflect: about the learner, about yourself and about the learning.

Chapter 7 contains rather more factual information than the other chapters because the area of special educational needs is surrounded by legislation, guidelines and special terminology. There are suggestions for ways of working with pupils who have specific learning difficulties and you may notice that they are very similar to suggestions made in earlier chapters for supporting learning in general.

Please read the book in the spirit in which it is intended: to help you to build on the experiences and expertise you already have by learning a little more about how learning happens and about some of the interesting developments in classroom practice that are helping our pupils, whatever their age and stage, to learn better.

1 What is Learning? How Does it Happen?

Chapter Outline

Three influential theorists

A theory of learning: social constructivism

Chapter summary

Learning involves all aspects of human development: physical, emotional, social and intellectual. (Ikin et al., 2000: 3)

In this chapter we are going to look at the work of three people whose ideas have influenced our understanding of how learning happens. We will go on to consider a theory of learning called social constructivism, which is built on some of the ideas put forward by our three influential thinkers and which can provide a strong theoretical basis to underpin classroom practice. To help us to see some practical applications of the theory we will use some classroom observations made by TA students during a professional development course, and during the chapter you will find suggestions for reflection and classroom based tasks to help your understanding.

Reflection

What do we mean by 'learning'? What does it involve? What do we need in order to do it well? Think about these questions and what they mean for yourself and for the pupils you work with. Jot down your thoughts and add to them as you work through this and later chapters.

Three influential theorists

Jean Piaget

Jean Piaget was born in Neuchatel in Switzerland in 1896 and spent most of his working life in Geneva. He was interested in how children develop their understanding of the world around them and he published an extensive range of books and papers over a period of forty years. Most of Piaget's books are available in English and titles such as *The Child's Conception of the World* and *Judgement and Reasoning in the Child* can be found in education department libraries. However, he is not easy to read, even in English, so it is a good idea to use one of the many books that summarize and comment on his work if you want to study his ideas further. Despite the difficulties of his language style and the fact that the ideas he was expressing were not in keeping with the traditional views of learning held at the time, Piaget's work has been, and continues to be, influential in our schools and particularly in Early Years education.

Some of Piaget's important ideas

> Intelligence is not created fully equipped, as if already contained in the organism, nor does it develop in a straight line but gradually built up stage by stage, each one beginning with the reconstruction of what has already been acquired at the previous stage. (Piaget, in Dixon, 2004)

1. Active construction of understanding

One of Piaget's most significant contributions has been the idea that intelligence is not simply the product of genetic inheritance but is something that is actively created by the learner through interaction with the environment. He observed his own children, at length, as they played and he watched how they tried things out and made mistakes; how they came to conclusions that, to adult eyes were correct or not. He decided that during play children were actively constructing their understanding of their environment by setting up hypotheses and testing them like scientists. Play, particularly when not over-directed by adults, is a cornerstone of the Piagetian approach to Early Years education.

Case study

The following case study is part of the evidence gathered by a TA for a course-work assignment. She was working on a module called 'How Children Learn' – part of a longer course. The task was to collect evidence of learning theories in action in the classroom.

Context

Reception class: observation of three children engaged in water play.

Summary of data	What this tells us about the children's learning	Link to learning theory
Children played well for about 10 minutes using the containers provided. They poured water from one container into another and talked about what they were doing. They used a range of mathematical language in a way that demonstrated their understanding.	Children were developing mathematical concepts by playing with appropriate materials and trying out different ways of using the equipment. They were also practising their use of mathematical language.	This links to Piaget's theory that children construct meaning by trying out ideas during play. Although the play materials had been provided by the teacher, the children were left to use them as they wanted.

2. Schema theory

Piaget believed that by interacting with the environment, in play or in the process of everyday life, children (and all human beings) develop concepts of how the world works. He called these concepts, or mental constructs, schemas. Schemas are the means by which the child makes sense of and organizes information about the world. Young children have the simplest of schemas, acquired through their immediate senses. A new experience is *assimilated* into an existing schema and in time becomes part of the child's thinking through a restructuring of that schema. The restructuring process is called *accommodation*. Assimilation and accommodation, the acceptance of new experiences and the modification of our ideas, are how human beings adapt to their environment: how they learn.

3. Stages of cognitive development

Piaget's close observation of children, at play and in what have been criticized as contrived test situations, led him to believe that the ability to think and learn develops through a series of stages as learners move from childhood towards adult reasoning. Piaget's stages are loosely age related and he believed that learners move through the stages in order – no one can skip a stage.

- **Stage 1: the sensori-motor stage**

  This stage lasts from birth to about 2 years of age. During this stage the child learns through movement and physical contact. Actions are initially uncoordinated but become more complex and organized and the child gradually becomes aware of the permanence of objects, for example that teddy doesn't cease to exist when he's hidden behind the cushion.

- **Stage 2: the pre-operational stage**
  This lasts from 2 years old to about 7 years old. Thinking in this stage is mainly based on intuition and immediate perception and is not necessarily logical. For example, the child could say that row A below contains more smiley faces than row B.
  Row A

  Row B

- **Stage 3: the concrete operational stage**
  This stage lasts from about 7 years old to about 12 years old. Children gradually become able to think more logically, especially about concrete and familiar situations.
- **Stage 4: the formal operational stage**
  This final stage is from about 12 years onwards. Children become increasingly able to think logically and to use abstract symbols and concepts. They are able to set up and test hypotheses and make deductions from evidence. This is the stage where adult reasoning begins.

There have been criticisms of Piaget's methods of generating data and the deductions he drew. Donaldson (1981) suggests that one of the main problems with Piaget's 'experiments' – the rather contrived scenarios he devised to explore children's thinking – was that he placed children in unfamiliar situations and asked them questions that did not make sense to them. Therefore, Donaldson feels, their actions and answers were unreliable. For readable accounts of Piaget's 'experimental' studies of children's thinking have a look at Davenport (1996) and for a critique of Piaget's studies see Donaldson (1981).

Lev Vygotsky

Lev Vygotsky was born in Russia in 1896. In his short life (he died of tuberculosis at the age of 38), he produced a body of work that has had a major influence upon developmental psychology and education. Under Stalin, Vygotsky's work and that of his colleagues was suppressed in the Soviet Union because it was deemed to be 'reactionary, bourgeois pseudo-science' (Palmer and Dolya, 2004). During the 1960s his works began to be available in translation and have been widely influential since then.

Some of Vygotsky's important ideas

> What a child can do in cooperation today he can do alone tomorrow. Therefore the only good kind of instruction is that which marches ahead of development and leads it. (Vygotsky, in Palmer and Dolya, 2004)

1. **Cultural tools**

   Vygotsky believed that the use of tools is a defining characteristic of human beings: it makes us different from animals. We have developed tools to help us physically and we have developed a range of what he called psychological tools to help us mentally. These psychological tools, such as symbols, numbers, pictures and most importantly language, help us to analyse and deal with the world around us; they are culturally determined and so they differ between cultures. We might say that they are 'cultural tools' and as such they need to be passed on from one generation to the next through education in its widest sense.

   For Vygotsky, educating children involves far more than furnishing them with a set of skills and a body of knowledge defined in a curriculum. Education means developing the ability to learn, an idea that is at the heart of many school-based projects and research activities at the moment. See Claxton (2002, 2004) and Cardiff Advisory Service for Education (2004). Vygotsky believed that the process of learning involves being able to think creatively, plan what to do and then be able do it. However, the process does not end with the 'doing' because an important part of learning is to be able to communicate what has been learned, in appropriate ways. The teacher's job is to provide children with the 'cultural tools' they need to be able to engage in the learning process effectively.

2. **Interrelationship of language and thought**

   At the heart of Vygotsky's thinking is the relationship between language and thought. He believed that thought is internalized language: think about adults 'thinking out loud' and children talking to themselves as they play. Externalized language in children becomes internalized as thought, though as adults we sometimes revert! If clear and creative thinking is important to the learning process and if language is fundamental to thinking, then it goes without saying that it is of great importance to develop children's linguistic abilities, both in terms of richness of vocabulary and range of expression.

Case study

This case study, like the one on page 8, was collected for the assignment on 'How Children Learn', by a different student on the same long course. This student has chosen to set out the notes in a different format.

Context

Year 3: observation of pair work.

Learning theory	Evidence and reflection
Talking helps to develop thinking (Vygotsky).	The children have been working on number bonds to 20 over a week. Today they were working in pairs, throwing 20 counters, which are red on one side and white on the other and counting the addition to find the number bond.
	Child 'A' has grasped the concept of using number bonds to solve an addition problem. He is talking to and showing child 'B' where in the sum the number bond occurs. Children 'C' and 'D' are working at the other end of the table. They have lost a counter so when they throw the bond does not work. They cannot see why the sum does not add up to 20. Child 'A' joins them and asks what the problem is. They look again at the counters and discuss what the task was and how they went about it. Eventually they realize that they have not got enough counters and that one has fallen on the floor. They carry on and child 'A' shows them how to use the number bond to complete their sum.

3. The social context of learning

Vygotsky, like Piaget, believed that children construct their own meaning but he differs from Piaget in that he stresses the importance of others in the process. Learning is very much a social and collaborative activity and the presence of others, both adults and peers, is vital. Also important is the context in which the learning takes place, which must be a meaningful one for the learner. The case study above is a good illustration of these factors, as well as a demonstration of the importance of talk.

4. Zone of proximal development (ZPD)

The zone of proximal development (ZPD) is a term coined by Vygotsky to describe the gap between what a child can do independently and what he/she can do with interested others: peers and adults. He believed that the teacher's role is to guide and support the child to work at the high end of her zone of proximal development, just beyond what she could do alone. Challenging but supported tasks promote the growth of understanding and working with others supports or 'scaffolds' the learner both emotionally and cognitively.

Case study

This is another example from the assignment on 'How Children Learn'.

Context

Year 4: design and technology, observation of individuals.

Learning theory	Evidence and reflection
Working in the zone of proximal development, learners support (scaffold) each other, emotionally and cognitively.	The children were working on various stitches while making an oven glove (blanket stitch, back stitch and running stitch). Child 'A' has finished his and is waiting for his next instruction. He notices that child 'B' is having difficulty with his blanket stitch and is becoming agitated. He approaches and tells 'B' 'Keep the line at the bottom straight, you're going wonky.' He stays with 'B' giving instructions verbally and visually until 'B' is able to work alone. He looks at me and says, 'My Nanna can sew, she showed me.'

5. **Metacognition**

   Vygotsky believed that there are two stages to the learning process. In the first stage the learner will learn about something or how to do something but will not be conscious that they know. In the second stage the learner will become increasingly aware that they know things but that there is more to know. This consciousness of learning and its process is called metacognition. The emphasis on reflection, which you will notice as you work through this book, is an indication of the importance attached to the awareness of learning in order to learn better, as a pupil in school or as an adult.

6. **Importance of play**

   For children in the early years Vygotsky believed that play provides the zone of proximal development. He wrote (in Palmer and Dolya, 2004), 'In play, the child is always behaving beyond his age, above his usual everyday behaviour. In play he is, as it were, a head above himself.' I'm sure we have all observed how absorbed children can be when playing, alone or with others. They concentrate longer, try out new things, rehearse what they know already, chatter constantly. Does this happen as much during directed tasks?

> **Task**
> Make a 5-minute observation of a group of children during directed and non-directed tasks. Make brief notes of what they do, what they say and how they interact. Reflect on your notes. Can you draw any conclusions?

Jerome Bruner

Jerome Bruner was born in New York in 1915 and throughout his long life has made major contributions to our understanding of teaching and learning in the classroom. He has worked in America and in the UK and is respected throughout the world. Bruner could be called the teachers' theorist as his ideas have been consistently grounded in classroom-based research and curriculum projects involving children of all ages, from pre-school to adolescence.

Some of Bruner's important ideas

- We begin with the hypothesis that any subject can be taught effectively in some intellectually honest form to any child at any stage of development.
- Knowing is a process not a product.
  (Bruner, in Wragg, 2004)

1. Stages of development

Like Piaget, Bruner believes that children's mental development progresses through a number of stages. These stages or phases are sequential but unlike in Piaget's theory, children do not leave one phase behind when progressing to the next. Rather, although there is a particular developmental stage where each phase tends to be dominant, Bruner feels that all the phases are used throughout our lives. Perhaps we could think of them as characteristic ways of thinking at different developmental stages, but not bound by ages.

Bruner identifies three stages:

- **The enactive phase**

  This is the earliest stage and corresponds to Piaget's sensori-motor stage. Thinking and learning are based on moving and manipulating: 'learning by doing'. Much of a child's learning and experience at this stage comes through playing.

- **The iconic phase**

  In this stage the learner starts to use representations such as pictures, numbers and diagrams as an aid to thinking and communicating.

- **The symbolic phase**

  The learner is now able to manipulate abstract concepts using more complex symbolism and language. This is the phase of adult reasoning.

We can all think of child and school related examples of these phases of thinking and learning but an illustration from adult experience shows how we can be operating in all three phases in different aspects of our lives. Imagine a theoretical physicist who spends most of her professional life working symbolically, using abstract concepts and language. She is obviously working here within Bruner's symbolic phase. At home she needs to put together a cupboard bought, in flat pack form, from a well-known furniture shop. She might think about it, try to visualize its construction and how she might put it together but she is most likely to look for the instructions and follow the diagrams (not always easy!). Here she will be working within Bruner's iconic phase. Later in the year she is planning to go skiing for the first time. She has spent a lot of time thinking about skiing and talking to friends about what is involved. She has also read books and looked at photos and diagrams. However, she will find that the only way to learn to ski is by actually doing it, working within Bruner's enactive phase, because the activity involves allowing the body to learn new skills and ways of moving that cannot be transmitted adequately through words, pictures or symbols.

2. **Construction of knowledge from past and present experience**

   Bruner believes that learning is an active process and that knowledge is actively constructed by the learner from a combination of past and present experiences. We might see some correspondence here with Piaget's schema theory. He developed a theory of curriculum, which he called the 'spiral curriculum', in which he suggested that topics and concepts should be introduced and then revisited to allow children to develop their understanding by building on what was already familiar to them. He was most careful, however, to stress that tasks must be presented in a way appropriate to the child's stage and always in a meaningful context.

3. **Importance of language and culture**

   Bruner was very much influenced by Vygotsky's work on language and culture and he came to believe that both were fundamental to what we learn and how we learn. As education professionals we need to pay great attention to children's language development, spoken as well as written, and we need to be aware of the culture in which learning is taking place. We can understand culture on several levels but for our purposes we need to be aware of the home cultures of our pupils, the prevailing culture in our communities and the culture of our school and classroom.

4. **Scaffolding**

   The term 'scaffolding' is widely used in education circles. The term was used by Bruner to describe the support given by adults, or by peers, when children are facing challenging tasks or coming to terms with new concepts and ideas. Bruner stresses the importance of the teacher in the learning process and says that scaffolding by interested adults can provide structures or connections that help the learner to persist and develop their understanding, rather than giving up because they 'don't get it'. We can link this idea to Vygotsky's zone of proximal development.

Case study

This is a fourth example from the assignment on 'How Children Learn'.

Context

Year 4, 28 children: observation focused on Ellie who has TA support in most of her lessons because of her learning difficulties.

Summary of data	What this tells us about the child's learning	Link to learning theory
Literacy lesson: The class teacher read through a poetry poster on the wall, the class then completed another poem together with the teacher on the board. The class then wrote their individual poems – Ellie looked relaxed and comfortable during the task and did not need any help from myself or the class teacher.	From the observation I saw that if a task is shared with the teacher first, then Ellie is far more likely to feel comfortable enough to complete it on her own without any further support.	This could link to Vygotsky's zone of proximal development. The teacher scaffolded the children's learning by modelling the process and the end product. Ellie could then do what she would not have been able to do by herself.

A theory of learning: social constructivism

Social constructivism is a set of ideas based on the theories of Piaget, Vygotsky and Bruner, which underpins much of the current thinking about how children learn and therefore what good classroom practice should involve. There are four basic principles, or key ideas, in the theory and Wray and Lewis (1997) explain them particularly clearly:

1. **Learning is a process of interaction between what is known and what is to be learned.**
   This key idea suggests that learning depends upon the learner already knowing something about the concept or subject matter to be learned. It also suggests that the learner needs to be aware that they know it. The teacher, therefore, needs to find out what the learner knows already, raise the learner's awareness and help the learner to make the connections between the old and the new.

2. **Learning is a social process.**
   Social interaction is an important part of the way in which human beings learn. The learner constructs their own meaning and understanding but does so in collaboration with and supported by others. When working with others a learner can work at a higher level by sharing the construction of knowledge and by 'borrowing' the understanding of other group members until

their own understanding is sufficiently developed. This principle requires us to provide well-organized group activities for our children; activities that necessarily involve discussion and interaction, not simply sitting together.

Case study

This is part of the case study used earlier. Here we are looking at Ellie working on a different task, which was to cut out shapes from a worksheet and rearrange them to make specific shapes.

Context:

Year 4, 28 children: observation focused on Ellie who has TA support in most of her lessons because of her learning difficulties.

Summary of data	What this tells us about the child's learning	Link to learning theory
Ellie tried to arrange the shapes without success. She said that it was hard. I (TA) reminded everyone that it was a group activity and that they work together and ask each other for help. Andrew offered to help and told Ellie that if she moved two shapes 'it would be OK'. Ellie tried this, commented that it wasn't quite right and then carried on moving the shapes until she made the correct shape.	Ellie was able to complete the task with help from a classmate where she could not do it by herself and might have given up. She was able to stick at the task and therefore, potentially, learn more.	Here we can see the social aspect of learning, in action. We have a child working within her zone of proximal development and being able to do something with others that she can't do by herself – she is borrowing someone else's skills or understanding while developing them for herself. Andrew is scaffolding her learning by demonstrating what to do (Vygotsky, Bruner, social constructivism).

3. **Learning is influenced by the context in which it takes place.**

   All learning is influenced by the context in which it takes place and for our children in school the context needs to be familiar and meaningful. We also need to be aware that skills and ways of working learned in one context may not be transferred easily to another context. The bar chart the child can construct in maths may not be so easy in geography and the exercises in thinking skills on Monday may have no discernible effect on the quality of thinking in science on Tuesday or history on Wednesday. The implication of this principle is that we must provide appropriate contexts for learning that take into account a child's cultural and linguistic background and that skills and concepts are taught in contexts similar to those in which they are to be used.

4. **Learning is a metacognitive process.**

   The key idea here is that good learners are aware of their learning and their level of under-standing. They are able to monitor the learning process, are aware when their understanding is incomplete and are also aware of what to do about it. We have all had the experience of the child who can read a piece of text seemingly perfectly and then be unable to say what it was about. Perhaps we have been in the same situation ourselves but then realized and reread the piece, paying attention this time! We, as adults, are more aware of our thinking processes and we need to help our children to become similarly aware. Ways of developing this awareness include the teacher modelling with a 'running commentary', encouraging children to think aloud as they work through a task and teaching children to reflect on what they have been doing and learning.

Chapter summary

In this chapter we have looked at the main ideas put forward by three very influential educational theorists: Piaget, Vygotsky and Bruner, and met the theory of learning based on these ideas: social constructivism. The four principles of social constructivist theory are:

1. Learning involves interaction between what is known and what is to be learned.
2. Learning is influenced by the context, emotional and cultural, in which it takes place.
3. Learning is a social process.
4. Learning involves metacognition.

These principles form the basis of what many see as teaching for good learning and they can be seen every day in our classrooms as the case studies provided by the TA students demonstrate.

> **Reflection and task**
> Reflect upon the chapter and try to make connections between the ideas of our three influential theorists and the theory of social constructivism. Try to do some short observations of groups and individual pupils and find some of these ideas in action in your classroom. Do you want to add anything to the notes you made at the beginning of the chapter?

2 Learning Styles and Multiple Intelligences

This chapter will focus on some of the factors that have an effect upon learning. We will discuss learning styles and multiple intelligences and go on to consider the importance of the emotional and social aspects of learning.

Reflection
Think about the pupils you work with. Have you noticed if any of them work better or are more engaged during some kinds of activities rather than others? How does their mood affect their willingness to learn?

Learning styles

What exactly do we mean by 'learning styles'? Most of us are familiar with the term. Staffroom and college library shelves are populated with books on teaching and learning that contain sections on preferred learning styles and tell us how important it is to identify and cater for the different learning styles of our pupils. Yet there is no reliable research-based evidence for the ideas being promoted.

There is no one definition of the term 'learning styles' but in schools we tend to use it to mean that there are a number of different ways of learning and that individual pupils will prefer to learn in some ways rather than others. Some of the many ideas relating to 'learning styles' are:

- Learning styles are the different ways of processing information – visually, aurally or kinesthetically.
- Learning styles are preferences for learning in a certain way, for example in a group or as an individual.
- Learning styles are different ways of going about tackling tasks and solving problems.

Some theories suggest that learning styles are permanent and 'built-in', so the learner will always prefer to learn in a particular way. Others maintain that experience, the environment and the type of activity will all influence the way learner sets about a learning task. See Becta (2005) for a short review of the related literature.

VAK

Perhaps the most widely known and used application of learning styles in schools is the concept of learning modalities. This theory suggests that all learners have a strong preference for learning through one or more of the sensory modalities: visual, auditory or kinesthetic. Therefore visual learners will learn best from written materials or pictures, auditory learners will learn best from the spoken word and kinesthetic learners will learn by being involved in movement and 'hands on' activities. The obvious problems here are that pupils could be labelled, which might result in restricting their learning experiences (I'm sure we have all heard or read that the majority of boys are kinesthetic learners) and that teachers will feel that they should be catering for the learning styles of 25 or so individuals.

Research, see Becta (2005), suggests that these preferences do indeed exist. However, there is no reliable evidence to show that a learner will have a strong preference for one learning style in particular and there is no evidence that matching teaching to an individual's preferred learning style is more effective than matching activities to the subject matter being taught. What does seem to be important is to provide pupils with a mixture of approaches to learning, to help them to become aware of the ways in which they learn best and to give them opportunities to think about, make decisions and talk about their learning.

Are learning styles helpful?

The idea of different approaches to learning can be used positively in our classrooms and can serve to remind us that our pupils learn best if they have a 'mixed diet' of learning experiences, including how we present them with information and instructions and the kinds of activities we involve them in.

Task

Make some informal observations and identify the kinds of activities that the pupils in your class are involved in. Does the mixture of activities involve opportunities to look or read? Are there opportunities to listen, not simply to the teacher, but to each other? Do some activities require bodily movement, or manipulation of equipment? Is one particular kind of activity used more than the others?

The following case studies are examples of lessons that demonstrate a 'mixed diet' of learning approaches. They were contributed by TAs as part of a professional development exercise. Are they like any of the lessons you have observed?

Case study 1

Curriculum Area	Pupils/Grouping	Timescale	Date	
Language/literacy	Reception: 8 boys, 4 girls, mixed ability	20–30 mins		

Resources: letter X story, X-ray, camera, egg timer, picture dictionaries, whiteboard, pens.

Activity	Learning outcomes	Notes/VAK
Introduction to letter X		
Children listen to true story about the teacher's daughter who broke her arm and had X-ray taken.	To be able to recognize the letter X.	Auditory
Children look at an X-ray of an arm and talk about it.		Visual
They then use a camera to pretend to take X-ray, making sure that they make the 'ks' sound as they take it.	To be able to say the letter sound.	Kinesthetic and auditory
The children choose talk partners for 3-minute timed activity to see if they could think of any words with X in them – picture dictionaries can be used.	To be able to recognize words that contain the sound X.	Auditory and visual
Plenary: collect the children's words on whiteboard; invite individuals to come up and underline the Xs in different colours.		Visual, auditory and kinesthetic
Conclude by writing the letter, saying it out loud and singing about it.		Auditory and visual

Evaluation/reflection
Children responded well and all were engaged and contributed throughout the lesson. Without prompting they were able to demonstrate using parts of their bodies: fingers, arms and legs to represent the letter. The variety of short activities involving speaking, listening, looking and moving contributed to the good learning.

Case study 2

Curriculum Area	Pupils/Grouping	Timescale	Date	
Science	Year 8: 8 boys, 14 girls; mixed ability groups already arranged	50 mins		

Resources: demonstration equipment, interactive whiteboard, sorting task (one envelope of pictures and texts per group).

Activity	Lesson objectives	Notes/VAK
• Write lesson objective in book.	Revise and consolidate understanding of scientific terms introduced in the previous lesson.	
• Teacher demonstration and explanation of keywords, followed by particular questions for each group.		Visual and auditory
• Interactive whiteboard demonstration of the processes shown in the demonstration; more questioning and discussion.		Visual and auditory
• Group sorting task: match picture to text. Then match to the correct definition on the board.		Visual, auditory and kinesthetic
• Pupils mark own work, after discussion of correct answers.		Auditory
• Plenary question and answer session.		

Evaluation/reflection
Multisensory teaching is evident throughout this lesson: visual, auditory and kinesthetic learning are all employed. All pupils appeared to be engaged in learning and there were no disruptive incidents.

Multiple intelligences

In 1983 Howard Gardner first published his theory of multiple intelligences. Since then he has continued to revise and extend his ideas, which have been taken up by teachers, schools and educational publishers and now inform a large body of curriculum programmes and resources. Gardner's theory, that there is not one but many intelligences, is very different from the view that informed much of twentieth century thinking about learning. The traditional view of intelligence is that each individual has a fixed amount of intellectual capacity that is a product of genetics and early environmental influences (nature and nurture). This is the kind of intelligence that is measured by IQ tests and is the basis for eleven-plus exams, and it is thought to remain constant and unchangeable.

Gardner's new idea was that there is a collection of different intelligences, perhaps groupings of abilities and aptitudes might be another way of expressing the idea, which we all possess to some degree and that can be developed further. The original seven intelligences are:

- linguistic: relating to language, written or spoken;
- logico-mathematical: relating to mathematical and scientific thinking and a structured approach to solving problems;
- visual-spatial: related to being able to visualize and manipulate images and understand spatial relationships;
- bodily-kinesthetic: relating to movement and the use of the body;
- musical: related to music, sound, rhythm;
- interpersonal: related to communicating, responding well to other people;
- intrapersonal: related to awareness and control of self.

A further intelligence, naturalistic: relating to the natural world and the environment, was added later. Gardner's view is that we all have all of these intelligences but we have them in different amounts and combinations that are not fixed but can be developed or diminished throughout our learning lives.

Can we use multiple intelligences to support learning?

As with learning styles multiple intelligences theory needs to be treated with care. If we try to profile our pupils and then teach strictly to their individual differences we run the risk of labelling them and restricting their learning. However, if we use the idea of multiple intelligences to expand both our teaching repertoire and our pupils' awareness of different ways of learning then we can support the development of independent and personalized learning. Multiple intelligences theory can make a useful contribution to the 'mixed diet' of experiences that we need to provide for our pupils and to the concepts and language that learners need in order to be able to reflect and learn about their learning.

> **Reflection**
> Think about yourself as a learner. Do you feel that you have a particular learning style? Do you recognize any of Howard Gardner's multiple intelligences in yourself?

Focus on learning

At the heart of recent developments in approaches to teaching and learning is the idea of 'learning to learn' (see Chapters 5 and 6). An important part of helping pupils to learn how to learn is giving them a framework and a language with which to think and talk about their learning. Learning styles and multiple intelligences can form a useful part of this framework for reflection about learning, just as they can inform teachers' planning by reminding us to organize a 'mixed diet' of learning experiences and offering our pupils choices about resources and ways of communicating their learning.

Social and emotional aspects of learning

The important role that the emotions play in every learning experience has been the subject of much recent research and discussion and, as we saw in Chapter 1, the social context of learning is very important. Therefore, before children can begin to tackle the cognitive demands of any task they need to be able to cope with the social and emotional demands that the activity makes. Of course, some of our pupils will have emotional difficulties beyond our control, which will interfere with their learning.

> The extent to which emotional upsets can interfere with mental life is no news to teachers. Students who are anxious, angry, or depressed don't learn; people who are caught in these states do not take in information efficiently or deal with it well. (Goleman, 1996: 78)

We won't be able to solve these problems but as educators we can be aware of the influence that emotion has upon learning.

What are the social and emotional aspects of learning?

A number of respected educational writers, including government advisory bodies, have written on the theme of social and emotional development and there is considerable agreement about the aspects of social and emotional development they think relate to learning.

Goleman (1996) has had widespread influence. He identified five components of what he called 'emotional intelligence':

- self-awareness
- managing emotions
- self-control/self-motivation
- empathy
- handling relationships/social arts.

Goleman maintains that these aspects of emotional development are more important to successful learning than the traditional intelligence measured by IQ tests.

Katherine Weare (2004), in her book *Developing the Emotionally Literate School*, talks about emotional literacy, which she defines as:

> the ability to understand ourselves and other people, and in particular to be aware of, understand and use information about the emotional states of ourselves and others with competence. It includes the ability to understand, express and manage our own emotions, and respond to the emotions of others, in ways that are helpful to ourselves and others. (Weare, 2004, in Claxton, 2005: 9)

The DfES booklet *Excellence and Enjoyment: the Social and Emotional Aspects of Learning*, written as part of the National Primary Strategy, contains information and guidance that can be applied to the secondary context as well as to the primary. The document identifies five social and emotional aspects of learning which it says 'underlie almost every aspect of school, home and community life, including effective learning and getting on with other people' (DfES, 2005a: 7). These aspects are:

- self-awareness
- managing feelings
- motivation
- empathy
- social skills.

Now let us try to make some connections between this part of the chapter and some of the ideas we have already met. The particular view of emotional intelligence, or emotional literacy, outlined above has its basis in Gardner's multiple intelligence theory. The two intelligences: interpersonal and intrapersonal, embrace the DfES social and emotional aspects and Goleman's five components of emotional intelligence. They can also be clearly seen in Weare's definition of emotional literacy.

Table 1: Social and emotional aspects of learning: drawing the links between Gardner, Goleman, Weare and the DfES

	Intrapersonal intelligence	Interpersonal intelligence
DfES: social and emotional aspects of learning	• self-awareness • managing feelings • motivation • *empathy	• social skills
Goleman: emotional intelligence	• self-awareness • managing emotions • self-control/motivation • *empathy	• handling relationships/social arts • *empathy
Weare: emotional literacy	• being aware of understanding and using information about our emotional states • expressing and managing emotions usefully	• being aware of, understanding and using information about the emotional states of others • responding to the emotions of others usefully

*You might feel that empathy could be both intrapersonal and interpersonal.

Reflection

The following activity has been designed to help you to reflect upon the idea of emotional intelligence and its different elements. It has been used in a number of teaching sessions with a variety of students, including TAs, and ideally should be done as a group, as the purpose of the activity is to stimulate thought and discussion about emotional intelligence rather than to present a set of facts. When done as a group the statements should be made into cards with one statement on each card. However, the set of statements can be used by individuals as a simple aid to reflection.

Emotional intelligence

This activity will help you to reflect on aspects of emotional intelligence. You will need to make a set of cards, using the statements below, which you can use either as an individual or with a group of colleagues.

Emotional intelligence involves two of Gardner's multiple intelligences:

1. intrapersonal intelligence: being aware of and being able to manage ourselves;

2. interpersonal intelligence: being able to relate effectively to other people.

Shuffle the statement cards and if you are working in a group deal them out. Read the statements and decide whether they give you information about intrapersonal or interpersonal intelligence. Sort the statements into intrapersonal or interpersonal and if there are some that you can't decide then place them in between.

Look at the statements for intrapersonal intelligence. How would you recognize pupils who are developing good intrapersonal intelligence?

Look at the statements for interpersonal intelligence. How would you recognize pupils who are developing good interpersonal intelligence?

Statements for the sorting cards

- Bonds with parents and interacts with others.
- Makes and maintains social relationships.
- Recognizes and uses a variety of ways to relate to others.
- Is aware of the feelings of others.
- Is aware that other people have different lifestyles and beliefs.
- Takes part in collaborative tasks.
- Takes on different roles, as appropriate, from leader to follower.
- Influences the opinions or actions of others.
- Understands and communicates effectively in both verbal and non-verbal ways.
- Is interested in careers such as teaching or social work.
- Is aware of their own different emotions.
- Can express their own feelings and thoughts appropriately.
- Is motivated to identify goals for themselves.
- Can work independently.
- Can identify and describe their own feelings.
- Can manage their own emotions.
- Can respond appropriately to the emotions of others.
- Can control their impulses.
- Can persevere with a task.
- Is honest and committed to justice/fairness.
- Can take responsibility for their actions.
- Is open to changing their behaviour and feelings.

- Is aware of themselves and their feelings.
- Is self-motivated.
- Can see other people's point of view.
- Can empathize with other people.
- Can handle relationships appropriately.
- Is aware of the effects of their behaviour on others.

Emotional intelligence in the classroom

The DfES booklet *Excellence and Enjoyment: the Social and Emotional Aspects of Learning*, referred to above, discusses why it is important to develop the social and emotional aspects of learning in the curriculum and tells us that learners who become 'emotionally intelligent' or 'emotionally literate' will:

- be effective and successful learners;
- make and sustain friendships;
- deal with and resolve conflict effectively and fairly;
- solve problems with others or by themselves;
- manage strong feelings such as frustration, anger and anxiety;
- be able to promote calm and optimistic states that promote the achievement of goals;
- recover from setbacks and persist in the face of difficulties;
- work and play cooperatively;
- compete fairly and win and lose with dignity and respect for competitors;
- recognize and stand up for their rights and the rights of others;
- understand and value the differences and commonalities between people, respecting the right of others to have beliefs and values different from their own.
  (DfES, 2005a: 7)

This sounds like the recipe for the perfect human being – a very tall order! Unfortunately, although there are appropriate support materials to be had, including the DfES guidance and SEAL project materials (DfES, 2005a), there are also some rather simplistic and poorly informed views of what teachers can do to help pupils to develop their emotional intelligence. Claxton (2005) gives a comprehensive and very readable critique of the research base for many of the ideas connected to emotional intelligence, including the view that high self-esteem always leads to better learning. The emphasis on self-esteem can lead to pupils being praised uncritically and perhaps inappropriately, and he cites research by Carol Dweck, an American psychologist, who says that 'self-esteem' is much more potent when it is 'won through striving whole-heartedly for worthwhile ends, rather than derived from praise', especially praise that may be only loosely related to actual achievement (Claxton, 2005: 17).

Claxton (2005: 31) concludes his overview of emotional intelligence by re-stating its importance and making recommendations, some of which you might like to consider, in your work as TAs:

- Modelling appropriate emotional responses may be more successful than simply discussing them, for example admitting to feeling grumpy or upset.
- Acknowledge pupils' emotions, don't react to them emotionally.
- Be critically aware of simple slogans and materials, including scientific claims made by non-scientists.
- Don't make assumptions about other people's emotions. People, children as well as adults, are complicated.
- Feelings are triggered by perceptions rather than facts so persuasion may not work.
- Habits will not be changed by a worksheet or a discussion. Awareness may be raised, but little more.
- Try to work on some of the counterproductive links between learning and emotion, for example:
  - Success means you are 'bright' (so failure means you are stupid, so don't attempt what you might fail at – in other words, don't take risks).
  - Speed of learning is an index of how 'bright' you are (so slow means stupid).
  - 'Bright' people find learning easy (so if you have to try, you must be stupid).
  - If you can't get it fast, you won't get it at all (so there is no point trying).
  - Learning is 'uncool' (so you risk being shamed or rejected if you look too 'keen').

Reflection

Think about Claxton's recommendations. Do you recognize any of the ideas in your own experiences? How do you feel about the 'counterproductive links'? Have you heard any of your pupils saying these things? Have you ever applied any of them to yourself?

Chapter summary

We have been looking, briefly, at learning styles, multiple intelligences and emotional intelligence. We have seen that although these theories are useful for us in the classroom we must treat them critically and use them to inform teaching and learning and not dictate it: they do have a part to play in the learning-centred classroom.

We will use the term 'learning-centred classroom' in later chapters and perhaps it may seem to be a truism that a classroom should be labelled as 'learning centred'. Surely every classroom is 'learning centred'? The answer to this question is 'yes, but some more so than others'. Hughes (1999) gives a lovely example of a 'perfect' lesson where a large notice is hung on the outside of the classroom door, at the beginning of the lesson, saying 'Do not disturb – learning in progress'. In a 'learning-centred' classroom the teacher pays careful attention to the learning environment (see Chapter 3) and all members of the class: pupils, teacher and support staff, are focused on learning.

A good environment for learning requires attention to the physical aspects of the classroom and also to the psychological and emotional aspects that comprise the classroom culture: 'how we do things here'. In a healthy, productive learning classroom all class members, pupils and staff, behave well to each other and respect each other's feelings, the aim being to work together in an atmosphere of mutual support and encouragement. Ginnis (2002: 25) tells us that 'everyone needs to feel emotionally secure and psychologically safe' and goes on to say that learning occurs most efficiently when the learner is not at all fearful of being bullied, ridiculed or ignored. This requires pupils to behave well to each other and teachers/staff to behave well towards pupils. The social and emotional development of the pupils is obviously of great importance in creating a good classroom culture: a complex enterprise and one that requires careful nurturing.

> **Reflection**
> Think about a classroom you work in. How do the pupils treat each other? Do they behave well towards the teacher? How do they behave towards you, as a TA, or towards other adults in the classroom? How do the adults in the classroom behave towards the pupils and towards each other?

3 The Learning Environment

All learners learn best in an environment that is comfortable, pleasant and well ordered. Our classrooms are where much of the learning in school takes place so the classroom environment must be carefully managed in order to encourage successful learning. The organization and management of the classroom are important parts of a teacher's planning: long term to build up an appropriate learning environment and culture, and short term when preparing specific learning experiences and activities.

> **Reflection**
> At the end of the last chapter you thought about one of the classrooms you work in and about the way in which pupils and adults behave towards each other. Think about that classroom again and try to identify any particular features of the classroom, and the way it is organized, that you think are particularly supportive and that help pupils to learn.

There are many important factors to consider in any well-ordered classroom but in this chapter we will consider four: the use of space, use of time, learning resources and the grouping of pupils for learning. How these factors are managed will differ according to the sector and type of school because, as you know, primary classrooms are usually managed differently from those in the secondary school and special school classrooms are uniquely organized for the specific needs of children involved.

The chapter makes use of materials and ideas produced by TAs working on a Foundation degree, which emphasizes learning together. In the taught sessions students work as a community of learners (see Chapter 5), sharing different experiences and areas of expertise and using their considerable knowledge of classroom practice as a foundation upon which to question and develop their understanding of children's learning.

Case study

The following activity was used during a college-based session on classroom management that focused on the four organizational factors we were considering: time, space, resources and grouping.

Students worked in four groups, each group comprising primary, secondary and special school TAs. The room was arranged into four workstations and at each station was a large piece of paper with either time or space or resources or grouping written on it. Each group was given a coloured pen, asked to appoint one member as a scribe and then had 5 minutes at one station where they wrote down everything they could about the organizational factor on their sheet. After 5 minutes the groups moved on to the next station where they added to, questioned or commented on the information already on the sheet. The process continued until the groups were back to the station at which they had started.

This initial activity elicited and acknowledged the experience the students already had and gave them the opportunity to share and question the ideas and practices from their different classrooms and settings. To extend their thinking each group was then given a number of short readings from books on classroom management and asked to use the information in the readings to supplement or change the information on their sheet. Finally they had to organize their information into a poster of what they considered to be the most important aspects of their organizational factor. The posters were displayed and time was made for the students to read them.

The feedback posters produced by the TA students will be used as a stimulus for further discussion and to raise some questions about the role of the teaching assistant in classroom management. It will be apparent as we go along that there is a great deal of overlap between the sections, for example the comments on time will involve consideration of resources and grouping, and the comments on grouping will involve consideration of space and so on. But that is the nature of the classroom and organizing learning.

Time in the learning environment

Information from feedback poster 1

The group that produced this poster decided to assemble their information under four headings: children's needs, time wasting, lesson time and balance.

1. Children's needs
- Children need personal time.
- Toilet time – absolute necessity for small children.
- Routines: break, story, lunch and so on give stable format to the day.

2. Lesson time
- Late arrivals upset the class for both teacher and pupils.
- Thinking and answering time is important.
- Appropriate time should be planned for different activities.
- Time should be built in for children's own interests.
- Appropriate extension work is needed for early finishers.
- Time is needed for specific subjects and literacy/numeracy.
- Time is needed for one to one sessions.

3. Time wasting
- Time is wasted if the teaching style/approach is not appropriate for the subject or the pupils.
- Time is wasted if resources are not prepared and ready.
- Time is affected by non-teaching activities.

4. Balance
- It is important to have right balance of theory and practical work.
- Imbalance can cause boredom or anxiety resulting in behaviour problems or 'switching off'.

Here we see number of useful observations about the use of time, some of which are primary school focused, but several apply to all educational settings. Let us consider the use of classroom time in a little more detail, using some of these points, under the headings of teacher time, pupil time and curriculum time.

a. Teacher time

Teachers invest a great deal of time in the planning and preparation of lessons. Much of this time is well spent but some, perhaps, could be more effective if better use were made of ongoing teacher assessment and helping children to become more confident and autonomous learners.

1. Assessment

Time is wasted when inappropriate activities or tasks are organized. Tasks can be too easy or simple, involving needless repetition, or lack of challenge, or low-level skills. Tasks can be too difficult, expecting pupils to use skills or knowledge they have not yet adequately developed. As we are all aware, easy tasks result in pupils 'finishing early' with the consequences of boredom or poor behaviour, or the need for extension activities. Are these extension activities sometimes more of the same and therefore contributing to boredom, or do they really stimulate and extend learning? Tasks that are too difficult often require constant repetition of instructions and explanations and are likely to involve pupils sitting with hands in the air waiting for help or 'switching off' altogether and having a chat with a neighbour. Good use of assessment information, gathered while talking to and observing pupils during lessons, helps teachers to plan the most appropriate tasks and activities for their pupils.

> **Question**
> To what extent do you, as a teaching assistant, monitor the learning of the pupils you work with and use that information to help plan work?

2. Autonomous (self-supporting) learners

A lot of classroom time, for teacher and pupil, is wasted in routine, organizational activities. The routines will be different in primary and secondary settings but the result is the same: erosion of learning time by low-level activity. By developing clear, learning-focused rather than behaviour-focused routines, a teacher can try to minimize the loss of learning time.

It goes without saying that resources must be prepared and ready for use but time spent establishing pupils' expectations of where to find instructions and materials and what to do when they arrive in class, is likely to be effective use of teacher time. Ikin et al. (2000) suggest using a 'jobs wall or board', where pupils choose from a list of ongoing tasks to occupy them for a short time while the administration is attended to. Tasks such as finishing off some work from the previous day, reading a chapter in book or finding out about something related to the current topic would be appropriate. This strategy works well in the primary setting and could be adapted to some secondary classrooms, particularly work with tutor groups.

Another simple but effective strategy was devised by a Cardiff teacher as part of an action research project into supporting learning. This particular classroom-based research project describes a routine developed with a Year 7 class that succeeded in reducing the time taken from coming into class to beginning the lesson from 15 minutes, which had been a cause for concern, to 5 minutes. The teacher worked with the class and together they discussed and developed an acrostic reminder poster (Cardiff Advisory Service, 2004: 119):

> **R**emove your coat and bags.
> **E**ating and drinking are not allowed in the classroom.
> **A**lways have your pen and planner with you for the lesson.
> **D**o calm down and BE STILL.
> **Y**ou are ready to learn.

It sounds rather obvious to say that a teacher's time is best spent teaching children. The demands of a class of pupils, whether primary or secondary, with its range of different needs, interests and aptitudes, means that a teacher can spend a lot of time on low-level maintenance and support rather than productively leading learning. Routines and strategies to help pupils support themselves and each other can help to give teachers the time they need to work intensively with individuals and groups. Self-sustaining group activities, with a clear expectation that the teacher will not be disturbed, can be used to good effect in both primary and secondary settings. Word banks, question walls and help posters are devices often used in primary classrooms and can be adapted for secondary classroom use. A range of simple strategies, including the one described above, can be found in the Cardiff Advisory Service (2004) publication *Learning to Learn: Enquiries into Building Resourceful, Resilient and Reflective Learners*. We will discuss some of these strategies further in Chapter 5.

> **Question**
> As a teaching assistant what routines could you develop to cut down on low-level maintenance tasks with your pupils, to make more time available for real learning?

b. Pupil time

How pupils use the learning time the teacher has planned for them will depend upon a variety of internal factors such as understanding, interest and motivation and external factors such as distractions, interruptions and lack of the right equipment. Good planning and a school and classroom culture that fosters a positive and resilient attitude towards learning will encourage pupils to make the most of their learning time, as will the routines and support strategies discussed above. Time spent by pupils in planning aspects of their own work and setting their own targets, even on an individual exercise or lesson basis, is pupil time well spent. Real involvement in the organization of their learning is motivating for pupils and encourages them to engage with the task, concentrate more and learn more.

In classroom discussions and in question and answer sessions pupils need time to think. Allowing thinking time before accepting answers is a way of slowing down those pupils who speak before they think and gives time for the less confident to marshal their thoughts so that they can make a contribution. Time to talk about and reflect on work and ideas is an important part of the learning process and therefore is an important use of pupil time. The reflection can be done as an individual, with a partner or group, or as part of a whole-class discussion but the thinking time is once again important.

> **Question**
> As a teaching assistant can you make the opportunities to give your pupils thinking time and planning time?

c. Curriculum time

We all grumble about the over-prescriptive and content-laden National Curriculum, which does not allow us time to develop topics in depth or to follow the pupils' interests. The curriculum is presently under review, which should result in less of a content burden. However, teachers have always had some discretion, particularly in the primary school, in the way they can combine subject areas and make the most of positive cross-curricular links. Literacy and numeracy are obviously of fundamental importance to all of our pupils and both can be taught and developed in a variety of interesting contexts and through the different curriculum areas. In the interests of needing time to improve their literacy and numeracy some special needs pupils experience a much reduced, and sometimes impoverished, curriculum because they are withdrawn from mainstream classes or given different work to do. Some EAL pupils also find themselves in this situation where they are treated as if they had a learning problem rather than a need to learn the language. We should be concerned to make sure that all pupils receive as broad and balanced a curriculum as possible and that reasonable time is given to a wide range of curriculum areas.

Question

As a teaching assistant what part can you play in ensuring that the pupils in your care enjoy a broad and balanced curriculum, as well as developing their basic skills?

Space in the learning environment

Information from feedback poster 2

Group 2, looking at the use of space in the classroom, also identified four main areas to consider: a general category, visual considerations, layout of the room and access issues.

1. **General**
   - The space needs to be safe, clean and warm.
   - It needs to be tidy and clutter on desks needs to be managed.
   - Wall space needs care and attention.
   - Music helps to provide a calm environment.
   - Windows are important for both ventilation and light – blinds can be an issue.
   - The classroom needs to be easy to maintain.

2. **Visual considerations**
   - Can the pupils see the teacher/board?
   - Can the teacher see the pupils?
   - Is there a focal point in the room?
   - Are the walls overcrowded?
   - What kind of displays are on the walls?

3. **Layout of the room**
   - 'Time out' space, quiet area, is a good idea.
   - Set areas for set activities, for example writing area.
   - Space is needed for practical activities.

- Personal space for pupils and teachers is desirable.
- Is the furniture arrangement flexible?
- The furniture needs to be appropriate for the age of the pupils.
- Room to move is important.
- Adequate storage space for books and materials is needed.

4. Access issues
- Room to move freely means that resources can be accessed.
- There should be no obstructions; clear entrances, exits, pathways around the room.
- SEN access must be considered.
- There should be access to outdoors for Foundation stage pupils.

As you can see from the feedback, our teaching assistants identified a number of very important factors to consider when thinking about the use of space in the classroom. I would like to extend the ideas a little by referring to the 'learning environment' rather than simply 'space' and add a few observations. First a general introductory statement from Dean (2001: 75):

> Children learn from the environment as well as from the teacher and each other, and the way the classroom is set up for learning is important. It should be attractive and welcoming but should have much available which encourages learning.

a. Wall space

The feedback poster mentions wall space twice. The walls are a very important part of the space in a classroom because they create the first impression of what goes on in the room and because they can do so much to link pleasant surroundings to active learning. All schools, secondary, primary and special, use their walls for displays of different kinds: important information and instructions; celebrating pupils' achievements of various kinds; displaying pupils' work. Ikin et al. (2000: 38) tell us:

> Display should be used to demonstrate high expectations, celebrate the achievement of all pupils, support and stimulate children's learning and reflect the whole curriculum.

Primary schools and secondary schools often have different needs and opportunities for classroom display. Secondary classroom displays will often be subject based, within departments; primary displays may also be subject based but within a single classroom and with more scope for cross-curricularity. Displays in special school classrooms will be tailored to the topic and the needs of the particular group of pupils based in the room; indeed in some circumstances it may be appropriate to have no displays at all.

We are all used to beautifully presented displays, assembled and constructed by the teacher, or by the TA, which show lovely examples of children's completed writing and drawing artfully arranged and enhanced by coloured card, paper, foil or fabric. These are welcome and enjoyable additions to our walls but do we stop to ask if the pupils actually notice them after a day or two?

Do they simply become wallpaper? Ikin et al. (2000: 38) encourage us to think of displays as resources for learning: ' to support and stimulate children's learning'. Dean (2001: 198) says that classrooms should be stimulating and '... display materials designed to set children thinking and asking questions ...' Let us think about displays that pose questions; that change and grow as the pupils ask and answer their own questions; that record the growth of knowledge and understanding as a topic progresses and that pupils are involved in making. There are some lovely examples of local studies displays and concept maps that work on these principles and it should be possible to produce them in the secondary setting as well as primary.

> **Question**
> To what extent do you influence wall displays in your classroom base, department or school? Could you involve some of the pupils you work with in making a display to record their learning in progress?

b. **Arranging the furniture**

The feedback takes full account of the importance of access, movement and working space. The teacher is responsible for the classroom layout and seating pattern and how she or he arranges the furniture and pupils will depend very much on their approach to teaching. A flexible approach to furniture arrangement is to be admired and encouraged but is often difficult in classrooms that are too small or that are used as routes to other rooms. The horseshoe arrangement of desks, not often used in primary schools but relatively common in the secondary sector, can give the flexibility for pupils to work in a variety of ways: individually, in pairs and groups and as a whole class, without having to move tables. Pupils can be very sensible when asked about their preferred seating arrangements and will have a view about the furniture and about the single or mixed gender seating arrangements – perhaps we could consult them more?

> **Question**
> To what extent do the classrooms you work in allow pupils to work in different ways: individually, in pairs, in groups, as a whole class?

Resources in the learning environment

Information from feedback poster 3

The feedback from group 3 was once more organized into four categories: quality, appropriateness, storage and accessibility.

1. **Quality**
   - Resources must be up to date.
   - They must be easy to keep in good order.

- They must be challenging, stimulating and imaginative.
- Quality must be good.
- Everyone must treat resources with respect.

2. **Appropriateness**
   - Resources should be attractive and pleasant to work with.
   - There should be a variety of different kinds of resources.
   - It is important that they are age appropriate.
   - There should be enough of them to go round.
   - They can be ability related.

3. **Storage**
   - Resources need to be stored safely.
   - They need to be clearly marked and perhaps colour coded.
   - They need to be managed and looked after – this needs to be someone's responsibility.

4. **Accessibility**
   - Resources should be easily accessible.
   - There are different requirements for basic resources and specialized resources.
   - There needs to be a clear system of access – classroom procedures.

Resources are servants not substitutes. (Laar et al., 1996: 33)

I like this quotation because it reminds us that a resource is only as good as the person who uses it. The teacher can make good use of a resource, a film for example, to stimulate discussion, raise questions and develop pupils' understanding or he or she can use it simply as a time filler.

The feedback shows us some important factors to consider when thinking about resources in the learning environment. Again, of course, the situation in secondary classrooms is often very different from that in primary, especially where access to basic resources like writing equipment is concerned and where reference materials are held outside the classroom in the school library. However, learning to choose and share resources is an important part of becoming the autonomous learner we are all trying to develop. Equally important is the responsibility for looking after and organizing classroom resources and respecting centrally held resources such as library books and specialized equipment. The points listed under 'quality' and 'appropriateness' are relevant in both settings, as they are in the special school.

As a teaching assistant you might be responsible for making specialized resources for the pupils in your care or you may work with teacher-made or published resources. Ideally you should be familiar with the resource you are using and you should be able to use it to enhance but not restrict your pupils' learning. The quality of the resource being used will have an effect upon learning but, as mentioned above, the way that it is used is also important. Consider the difference between using a double page spread in a KS3 history text book as a worksheet to be completed individually, and using it to raise questions and stimulate a group discussion, followed by some individual or paired writing based on the questions asked in the text. The second approach would necessarily require preparation but the learning is likely to be better.

> **Question**
> Do you always know what has been planned for lessons, so that you can prepare any resources you might need?

Grouping for learning

Information from feedback poster 4

The feedback from this group was set out in five sections: general, specialized needs, individual, paired and groups.

1. **General**
   - The grouping must be fit for purpose and it is an opportunity for the teacher to organize best layout and way of grouping.
   - Classroom geography plays a part; the furniture and the size and shape of the room have an influence.
   - Seating plans are important but a boy/girl seating plan is not always suitable.

2. **Specialized needs**
   - Hearing and visually impaired may need special arrangements.
   - Physical needs must be considered, for example wheelchair or special chair access; left-handed learners.
   - Language needs must be considered, for example EAL learners.

3. **Individual**
   - Some pupils need one to one teaching – child and TA, or teacher.
   - There needs to be opportunity for individual work.

4. **Pairs**
   - Sometimes it is good to work with a friend.
   - There should be opportunities to work with classmates other than friends.
   - A 'buddy system' is good support for newcomers and an opportunity for older and younger pupils to work together.

5. **Groups**
   - There can be different activities for different groups: differentiated curriculum.
   - Mixed ability groups allow for leaders and followers. They provide scaffolding and encourage the development of interpersonal skills.

- Same ability groups allow pupils to work at the same level, perhaps faster or slower than other groups.
- Mixed age groups allow older pupils to model appropriate behaviour for younger children.
- Friendship groups allow pupil choice. Sometimes this works well but not always. It creates security for some children.
- Behaviour related grouping allows the teacher to separate pupils who clash.

Hayes (2001, Chapters 5 and 6) makes the distinction between efficient and effective teaching. Efficient teaching refers to the technical aspects of teaching, such as resources, organization and general behaviour management, which might be acceptable even in cases where the learning is not very good. Effective teaching refers to lessons where the pupils learn well what the teacher expects them to learn. The idea of efficient and effective can be applied to ways in which we group our pupils for learning. As we can see from the feedback poster our teaching assistants have a good awareness of the different ways of organizing pupils and some of the factors to be considered when grouping pupils for learning.

The first general point is the one of overarching importance: fitness for purpose and the opportunity for the teacher to organize the best layout and way of grouping. 'Best' in this case means most effective for learning: will the pupils learn best as individuals, in pairs, groups or as a whole class? Should they have opportunities during the lesson to learn in a variety of groupings, for example starting off as a whole class, then working in pairs, then as an individual and finally as a whole class again? Who should be paired with whom; how should the groups be made up?

It is important, at times, for pupils to work as individuals and as teaching assistants you will often be called upon to support and work with individual pupils. It is worth considering seating arrangements when pupils are expected to work individually: it is difficult to concentrate and work on your own if you are looking at someone else across a table, or if someone on your table is working with a teaching assistant.

Much primary school work is nominally 'group-work': pupils are seated around tables to do their work and they are able to share and talk about what they are doing. The group-work is often efficient in terms of pupil management and teacher time as it can allow the teacher to spend time on in-depth work with a group, but it can be ineffective in terms of genuine learning because the remaining groups may be working on undemanding, self-sustaining tasks that do not challenge and do not develop pupils' learning. Work that is genuinely collaborative and that requires contributions from all members of the group to a shared product is more demanding to organize but can be much more effective in terms of learning.

Question
How can you, as a teaching assistant, encourage the pupils you work with to work collaboratively in pairs or in small groups?

Effective learning requires opportunities for interaction with others, adults and peers, in order to talk, question and reflect. When we group our pupils for learning we should be trying to provide them with opportunities for good quality interactions that will develop their skills and understanding. Sometimes these interactions will be with peers: friends, randomly chosen classmates, carefully chosen classmates, younger or older pupils in the school. Sometimes they will be with adults: teacher, teaching assistant, other adults in the room. The teaching assistant can play an important role in supporting the quality of the interaction, and therefore the quality of learning, in different situations both on a one to one, adult/child basis and when encouraging peer interaction in a group.

Chapter summary

In this chapter we have looked at four very basic aspects of classroom management and organization that make important contributions to a good learning environment.

We have used the knowledge and experiences of a group of TAs to guide a short examination of the use of time, space, resources and grouping for learning. You have been encouraged to look at your own classrooms and to question how you might manage these aspects of management in your work.

Reflection
Look back over your answers to the questions you have been asked during this chapter. Choose one or two to think about in more depth and take action upon, perhaps involving your teacher colleague.

4 The Learning Cycle: Planning and Assessment

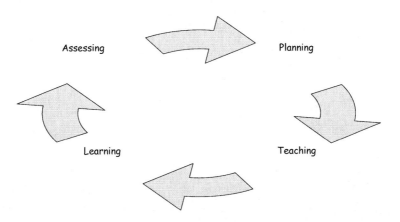

Figure 1: The learning cycle

The diagram above shows us a simple model of a complex process: that of organizing learning using the cycle of planning, teaching, learning and assessment. This chapter will focus on two important elements of this 'learning cycle' and, as in previous chapters, we will use TA students' responses and examples from some assignments to illustrate some of the ideas we discuss.

Question
To what extent are you, as a TA, involved in planning lessons?

Why is it important to plan?

Effective planning ensures coherent sequences of well-structured activities that are appropriate for the pupils involved. It also means that resources are more likely to be used efficiently. All teachers need to plan, even those with many years of experience. Plans do not need to be reinvented each year but they do need to be adapted in the light of different groups of children, new ideas and new resources. Plans, particularly medium-term plans, need to be flexible and adaptable, as Table 2 suggests.

Table 2: Approaches to planning

RIGID PLANS	FLEXIBLE PLANS	NO PLAN
• Can mean loss of spontaneity and enthusiasm. • Opportunities may be missed. • Pupils' learning (pace, understanding) is not adequately considered.	• Can provide a clear framework with identified units of work but some 'built-in slack' can allow for response to topical events. • Clearly defined learning outcomes mean that suggestions for activities in schemes of work should be just that – suggestions.	• Allows for spontaneity and response to topical events but does not take account of pupils' entitlement to a broad and balanced education.

Levels of planning

Medium term

This level of planning has many different names. Some schools have 'schemes of work', some have term or half-term plans, some have module or topic or unit plans. The name is not important but the principle of this level of planning is very important to the continuity and coherence of pupils' learning as it provides an overview of a sequence of lessons and intended learning outcomes.

The following principles of medium-term planning, some from Clarke (2001), are intended as suggestions for what should be considered at the medium-term planning stage.

• Broad learning intentions should be defined at the outset and should be a menu for a unit of work.

- You do not require the same amount of time for each learning intention.

- Aim for small number of activities linked to group of learning intentions.

- Think about a variety of activities and pupil groupings across the unit of work.

- Identify any important resources, visits, visitors.

Short term

Short-term plans are the daily or weekly plans made for immediate classroom use. There are many ways of writing these and each school will have its preferred planning format. At this level the following principles should be considered.

- There should be clear learning intentions for each lesson/session – this is the starting point because if you are clear about what you want the pupils to learn you are more likely to organize an appropriate activity or exercise.

- There should be sufficient detail in the activity to be useful – it is a working document.

- Consider differentiation at this stage: are all the pupils in the class able to access the learning?

- Have a space for assessment jottings – these will inform future planning.

> **Task**
> Talk to a teacher colleague about how she or he does short-term planning. Is there a preferred planning format for use in the school or department, or can colleagues make up their own?

Assessment

> **Question**
> What do we mean by assessment? Think about this question and jot down a few ideas. Come back to your jottings at the end of the chapter and see if you want to add or change anything.

We are all familiar with the term 'assessment' and should be aware that there are different approaches to assessment for different purposes. You will probably have met the terms 'summative assessment' and 'formative assessment', which are the main forms of assessment we use in education. Summative assessment is the assessment *of* learning and takes place after something has been taught, whereas formative assessment is assessment *for* learning and takes place on a daily basis, as part of the teaching and learning process.

> If we think of our children as plants ... **summative** assessment is the process of simply measuring them. The measurements might be interesting to compare and analyse, but, in themselves, they do not affect the growth of plants. **Formative** assessment, on the other hand, is the garden equivalent of feeding and watering the plants – directly affecting their growth. (Clarke, 1998)

GCSEs, SATs, end of year tests and weekly spelling tests are examples of summative assessment, as are end of year teacher assessments. Our discussion will focus on formative assessment (assessment for learning) and its importance in the teaching and learning process. We will also consider the role that TAs play in assessing pupils' learning.

What is the purpose of assessment?

The following list shows some of the ideas contributed by TAs during a CPD course. The question they were asked to consider was 'What is assessment for?'

- enhance pupils' learning
- check teaching objectives against learning outcomes
- recognize and plan for pupils' learning needs
- discover what pupils know, understand, can do
- help plan future learning
- help pupils devise personal targets
- evaluate teacher effectiveness
- help teachers to understand how pupils' learning is progressing
- guide teachers' response to pupils' learning
- help to raise pupils' achievement
- provide information for parents and for other teachers.

The list shows a good appreciation of the complex reasons for assessment and an understanding of the range of people interested in assessment information: pupils, class/subject teacher, next year's teacher, parents. Of course, the list can be extended to include head of year, form tutor, headteacher, SENCO, Ofsted/Estyn inspector.

In answer to the question 'What do we assess?' the TAs made the following list:

- understanding of task
- how pupils interact

- how pupils progress through a task
- how they are learning
- what they are learning
- how well they are learning
- if they are learning what we want them to learn
- what they are not learning
- what they do not understand
- when to intervene
- whether to intervene or not
- what they have understood
- what they can remember
- what they know already.

Question
Can you add any other purposes and focuses for assessment to the lists?

The place of assessment in the classroom

Figure 1 on page 39 is a simple demonstration of the process of organizing teaching and learning. The intention is to show that teaching and learning depend upon planning, which depends upon assessment. However, a good teacher constantly assesses her pupils and adjusts her teaching in the light of how the pupils are learning. These adjustments may come during the lesson, and as such they are unplanned, or they may need a change in the planning for future lessons. The constant 'fine-tuning' that goes on in the process of a lesson does not show up in our diagram. Ongoing teacher assessment, used to inform planning and classroom practice, is what we call 'assessment for learning' or formative assessment and we need to be clear about how we can make it become an integral part of the teaching and learning process.

A number of important characteristics of assessment for learning have been identified through extensive classroom-based research and you will find them in many recent books on the basics of organizing teaching and learning, and on teacher support websites such as the QCA website. In particular Black et al. (2002, 2003) and Clarke (1998, 2001, 2003, 2005) have made important contributions to our understanding of how assessment can help learning.

Some characteristics of assessment for learning

- Importance is placed on planning and the clarification of learning intentions at planning stage.
- The learning intentions are shared with the pupils.
- Pupils' learning is monitored while in progress.
- Oral and written feedback is given, focused on the learning intentions.
- Pupils are encouraged to evaluate themselves and each other, using the learning intentions.
- Individual target setting involves collaboration between teacher and pupil.
- Pupil self-esteem is raised because pupils are actively involved in the learning process.

> **Question**
> As a TA you will be involved in some of these aspects of assessment for learning. Which aspects are you involved with on a daily basis?

Let us explore these characteristics in a little more depth.

The importance of planning and the clarification of learning intentions at planning stage

Planning is usually the responsibility of the teacher but increasingly TAs are becoming involved in planning for the groups of children they work with. If we are clear about what we want the children to learn we are better able to organize tasks and experiences that will support that learning. Planning will take account of what we know already about our pupils' learning, and will include notes on appropriate differentiation strategies to cater for their needs. Of course, we cannot guarantee that our pupils will learn what we want them to but if we have a clear idea of what we intend them to learn then we will be better able to evaluate the effectiveness of our teaching as well as our pupils' learning. On a purely practical note the clear learning intention will give us a clearer focus for marking and feedback.

Sharing the learning intentions with the pupils

Many of you will be familiar with this idea and will be working in classrooms where the teacher uses 'WALT' – 'we are learning to' – at the beginning of a lesson. It will usually be necessary to explain the learning intention in 'childspeak' and often WALT will be prominently displayed in the room and read out loud by one of the pupils. It is also useful to explain to pupils why they are learning this and what they need to do to show that they have learned it (success criteria).

Of course, we can be flexible about when we share the learning intentions. No one would want to spoil a good story or a really stimulating start to a lesson, so sometimes it will be appropriate to discuss the learning later.

Why should we share learning intentions with the pupils?

There are several very practical reasons for sharing learning intentions with pupils. According to Clarke (1998), sharing learning intentions:

- transfers some responsibility for learning to pupils and they become active participants rather than passive recipients;
- pupils are more likely to achieve the learning objective if they are clear what they are aspiring to;
- pupils are more likely to focus on the purpose of learning rather than completion of the activity;
- pupils are more likely to stay on-task and refine work to match the learning objectives;
- pupils have a tool for evaluating their own learning.

Monitoring pupils' learning in progress

Question
How can we find out what pupils are learning? Jot down some of the things you do to find out if and what pupils are learning.

a. Observation

The strategy that most of us use most of the time is watching pupils and listening to their discussions as they work. This gives us valuable clues about how learning is progressing, as it is happening. We can also do planned observations on individuals and groups of pupils who might have particular needs.

Case study

Context

Year 7: food technology class. Mixed ability group.

Observation data	What this tells us about the child's learning	Comments
The class was asked to draw a cross section of the cake they were going to make. Tom was unsure of how to do this, turned to Jessica behind him and asked to look at her work to see what he had to do.	Tom needed a little help to get started on the task. Instead of wasting time and waiting for the teacher he turned to a classmate for help and both pupils were happy to work collaboratively.	Tom did not understand initially – why? Unclear explanation? Not listening? His attitude to learning was good as he was prepared to ask Jessica for help. If he had been required to work alone he would not have completed the task. Tom and Jessica work well together, perhaps they could be paired up more often.

The TA who collected this observation data was able to reflect and comment on Tom's learning. She raised some questions for herself about the reasons why Tom could not start the task and then she commented on his attitude to learning and a strategy to support his learning in the future: to work more often with Jessica. The observation enabled her to see how Tom was managing his learning.

b. Questioning

There are several stages in a lesson when it is useful to ask questions: at the beginning, to establish an appropriate starting point; during work, to check understanding and recall; when pupils are stuck in order to tease out the reasons for the problem; at the end also to check understanding. It is important that all pupils are involved in the questioning process and have the opportunity to answer questions. However, it is often the case that some pupils dominate classroom discussion while others take a back seat and participate as little as possible. As education professionals we need to encourage good pupil response to discussion and questions and we need to develop strategies that enable all our pupils to participate, at the level at which they feel comfortable. There are several simple strategies that can be used to slow down the response time, and encourage thinking and participation such as those found in Black et al. (2002) and Clarke (2001):

- 'Wait time' – insist that pupils wait before responding. This gives time for thinking and encourages a better quality response than one which comes 'off the top of my head!' Some pupils like to think through an answer before they are willing to put up their hands and are therefore at a disadvantage if the teacher expects answers to be given quickly.
- Ask pupils to discuss possible answers in pairs before putting up hands. You could use this strategy with the one above and it will encourage all pupils to participate in the thinking.

- Give pupils a choice between two or more possible answers and ask them to vote. Again, this will encourage thinking and participation.
- 'No hands up' rule – everyone is expected to be able to give an answer, even if it is 'I don't know'.

Other ideas to encourage pupils to extend their answers and comments include:

- Using non-verbal invitations such as eye contact, head tilt, nod.
- Inviting pupils to elaborate on their initial answer, for example *'Can you say a little more about ...?'*
- Adding something from your own experience, for example *'I remember when ...'*
- Clarifying ideas, for example *'I can tell this is the case because ...'*
- Echoing the answer, for example *'So you think that ...'*
- Making a suggestion, for example *'Perhaps you could try ...'*
- Reflecting on the topic being discussed, for example *'Yes, I sometimes think that ...'*
- Speculating on the topic, for example *'What if ...?'*

c. How do you know when they know it?

It is not always easy to know when a pupil really understands but with a combination of observing and questioning you can collect the information you need to make an informed judgement.

When you are observing, look for:

- Changes in body language and demeanour. Are they 'bright-eyed or half-hearted'?
- The ability to focus their attention. Persistence is a sign of understanding.
- The ability to modify what they are doing. Those who understand make their own modifications or try a different approach while those who don't will copy or follow instructions.
- The ability to use short cuts, which indicates that they can see the 'bigger picture'.

Task

When you are discussing work with pupils and questioning them include the words 'do you think' in questions and leave a 5-second wait time to encourage them to think. Look for the ability to explain and also to extend the concept. Those who have understood can often take the idea further on their own.

Oral and written feedback focused on the learning intentions

Question

Marking pupils' work and giving them feedback is part of everyday classroom life. As a TA are you involved in marking and giving feedback? What is your school policy on marking and feedback? Do you use marks or grades, or do you simply make comments, or do you use a combination of marks and comments?

Research (for example in Clarke, 2005) shows that making comments on pupils' work enhances learning and also improves pupils' engagement with their work. However, if grades are given as well as comments then pupils tend to ignore the comments and only focus on the grades. This is obviously not a productive use of the teacher time spent writing the comments! So how can we use marking and feedback to improve our pupils' learning? There are several important steps that apply, whether the feedback is going to be oral or written:

- Feedback needs to be based on clear learning intentions, which the pupil knows.
- Successes, linked to the learning intentions, need to be shown. For example, underline or highlight three places where the pupil has met the learning intention.
- It is important to show where improvement could take place, again by underlining or by using a symbol such as an asterisk or an arrow.
- It is important to show how the improvement could be made. This could be done orally by asking the pupil for suggestions for improvement, or in writing. The Primary National Strategy (DfES, 2004) suggests three types of improvement prompt which can be used effectively with all pupils:
  - a reminder (of the learning intention)
  - scaffolding (giving examples of what they need to do)
  - an explicit example (giving the exact word, sentence or process which the pupil can then copy).
- Time needs to be allocated for pupils to read or talk about the feedback and, very importantly, time also needs to be allocated for pupils to make the improvement. Feedback and improvement time would give useful opportunities for the TA to work with individuals or small groups of pupils to help them to work with the feedback comments.

Pupil self- and peer evaluation

Self-assessment, helped by peer assessment, plays an important part in enhancing learning. Self-assessment is not an easy process: pupils need to be given opportunities to review their learning and help to develop the skills they need in order to reflect productively. Peer assessment, in pairs or small groups, can help pupils to develop these skills, see Black et al. (2002); Clarke, (2003, 2005).

In Chapter 2 we discussed the social and emotional aspects of learning and in Chapter 5 you will find a discussion about 'learning to learn' and 'communities of learning'. Pupil self- and peer assessment has links to both of these topics because the process of evaluation of oneself and of others requires the development of inter-personal and intrapersonal skills (see Chapter 2). This process is also an important feature of 'learning to learn' in a supportive 'community of learners' (see Chapter 5).

How can we support self- and peer assessment?

We can do a number of things to help our pupils to learn how to assess themselves and each other.

- We can encourage pupils to evaluate/mark their work against learning objectives before handing it in for marking.
- We can encourage a safe and non-threatening classroom culture – absolutely essential for peer assessment. The focus must be on learning, not on persons.
- We can provide pupils with questions they can use to assess themselves, for example:
  - Were the learning objectives clear?
  - What did you find easy about the task or lesson?
  - What did you find difficult and what helped you move on?
  - What do you need more help with?
  - How would you change this activity for another group to do?
- We can model answers to these questions while pupils get used to using them independently.
- We can provide opportunities for evaluation at the end of lessons.
- We can allow pupils time to become used to the approach. It takes time to get used to a new way of working, especially if marks or grades are not used, and time to develop the skills and attitudes needed for this to be a valuable process.

Individual target setting involving collaboration between teacher and pupil

Target setting is not the same as setting the learning intentions for the lesson. Personal targets run alongside the learning intentions and work best if they are based on pupils' actual achievements. Both teacher and pupils need to be involved in the target setting process, which is part of the wider process of self-assessment.

There are several reasons for setting personal targets with our pupils. Clarke (2003) tells us that:

- they give a focus for teachers and pupils to monitor progress in specific areas;
- the process involves pupils in assessment and enables them to be active participants in learning;
- the process helps to make progress visible to the pupils themselves and to others. It can also increase the rate of progress;
- the process promotes self-esteem and motivation, probably because of the active involvement and the visible progress.

She goes on to say that personal targets are particularly effective when they are:

- framed as learning targets in language pupils can understand;
- based on evidence from feedback or marking;
- related to individual needs;
- just within the grasp of the individual pupil, that is challenging but achievable;
- in front of pupils when they are doing their work – many schools use individual target cards;
- fairly short term;
- set and signed off in negotiation with pupil.

> **Question**
> To what extent are you, as a TA, involved in target setting with the pupils in your care?

Pupil self-esteem is raised

As we have seen in earlier chapters learning is a complex process that involves a whole host of factors such as context, emotion and motivation, as well as cognitive skills and abilities. Studies such as those in Black et al. (2002) and Clarke (2005) show that actively involving pupils in their learning, by using the assessment and feedback strategies discussed above, can increase the motivation and self-esteem of all pupils, especially the low achievers. These strategies focus on effort and improving learning rather than on ability and give all learners guidance on how to improve. This kind of guidance has a motivating effect rather different from the often damaging effect that constant low grades can have on the low-achieving pupil.

Finally

Improving learning through assessment depends on five factors:

1. Teaching is constantly adjusted to take account of results of assessment.

2. Pupils are actively involved in their own learning.

3. Effective feedback, written and oral, is given to pupils.

4. Pupils are given opportunities to assess themselves and understand how to improve.

5. It is recognized that assessment has a profound effect on the motivation and self-esteem of pupils – both crucial to learning.

> **Question**
> Do you want to add anything to the jottings you made at the beginning of the section on assessment?

> **Task**
> Collect examples of comments, written or spoken, you could use to give feedback to your pupils. Make some comments about success and some to suggest improvements.

Chapter summary

In this chapter we have considered two of the elements of the learning cycle: planning and assessment. Important points to remember include:

1. Good planning, flexible and adaptable, underpins good teaching and learning.
2. Assessment for learning underpins good planning.
3. Assessment for learning involves both teachers and pupils.
4. Assessment for learning has positive effects on self-esteem and motivation because pupils are actively involved in their learning.

5 Learning to Learn

Chapter Outline

Thinking about learners and leaders

Learning-centred classrooms and communities of learners

Communities of enquiry

Dialogic teaching: learning through talk

Teaching pupils to be learners: learning to learn

Bringing it all together: reflection on the case study

Chapter summary

In this chapter we will build on some of the ideas introduced at the end of Chapter 2, where we talked about 'learning-centred classrooms', and Chapter 3, where we introduced the ideas of 'communities of learners' and 'learning to learn'.

Thinking about learners and leaders

In a busy school and classroom it is easy to make the simple assumption that the teacher leads the learning, helped by the TA, and the pupils do the learning. However, with a little reflection we can see that the situation is not really as simple as that.

Reflection
Think about the different aspects of your busy lives, in and out of school, and try to identify situations in which you are (a) a learner; (b) a leader of learning for others.

Some suggestions given by TAs in a recent discussion were:

TA as learner	TA as leader of learning
• When enrolled on a course, for example A levels, Foundation degree, other accredited courses. • When involved in any professional development opportunity, in or out of school. • In discussion with colleagues, teachers and TAs, in own school and other schools. • From the teacher, during a lesson, along with the pupils. • From the pupils: abilities, interests, progress, 'what works'.	• Working with individuals, groups and whole classes during lessons. • Working with support groups, nurture groups and target groups of pupils. • Advising and demonstrating strategies to colleagues. • Using open-ended questions with pupils and giving them time to think before answering. • Providing a rich, 'enhanced' environment at Foundation stage. • Modelling responses and behaviour for pupils. • Mentoring pupils and colleagues.

Question

Can you think of any examples where pupils lead the learning?

Suggestions made by TAs in the same discussion were:

Pupils as leaders of learning
- during role play/drama
- during free play
- during peer assessment
- when sharing ideas in paired or group-work
- when choosing own resources or way of presenting information
- in a properly run school council
- as part of a 'buddy' or peer mentoring system.

Learning-centred classrooms and communities of learners

In many of our classrooms, primary and secondary, there has been a shift of emphasis recently from a focus on effective teaching strategies to a focus on effective learning. In these classrooms, which Watkins (2003) refers to as 'learning-centred classrooms', there is more of a shared relationship between teacher and pupil, greater emphasis on building understanding and greater pupil responsibility for learning. In this kind of classroom all members are encouraged to see themselves as part of a community of learners rather than as a group of individual learners. The roles of learner and leader of learning are more flexibly applied than in a more traditional classroom: teacher, TA and pupils will all be learners and leaders at different times, depending upon the learning activities organized. This is not to say that the classroom teacher is not the manager of the pupils' learning because, of course, the responsibility for organizing the learning environment and learning opportunities, including the planning we referred to in Chapter 3, rests with the education professionals: the teacher and the TA.

Some of the features of the classroom as a community of learners, identified by Watkins (2001) in research conducted at the London University Institute of Education, are interesting and thought provoking. You might want to consider if you recognize any of them in your own classroom.

Some features of the classroom as a community of learners
- Social and *learning* relations between pupils are built up.
- Dialogue between pupils is encouraged.
- Collaborative learning approaches are used.
- A sense of belonging is promoted.
- There are opportunities for pupils to participate and to make choices.
- Pupils have opportunities to work in small, mixed ability groups.
- Pupils are encouraged to reflect on their learning.
- Pupils are given opportunities to ask questions and to follow them up.
- Writing is used as a tool for learning, not simply to provide evidence.
- Emotional intelligence is promoted.

Let us consider some examples of learning communities so that you can see some of these ideas in action.

Communities of enquiry

Some of you may be familiar with Philosophy for Children, or P4C, an approach that is widely used in primary schools and is beginning to find its way into secondary schools. P4C is based on the idea of a community of enquiry and it essentially involves a group of people who come together to raise questions, of a philosophical rather than a factual nature, and to collaborate as they think and reflect. The questions for discussion are chosen by the group, in response to a stimulus such as a story or a picture, and members are careful to observe particular rules so that the discussion can proceed productively. Examples of rules are:

- all contributions are valued

- all participants are respected

- participants give reasons for what they say.

This approach necessarily involves a shift in roles between teacher and pupils, even with the youngest children, because although the teacher may introduce the stimulus and encourage the members of the group the pupils decide upon the questions and the direction of the enquiry. Thus the role of leader of learning is passed back and forth between pupils and teacher, or other adult. The adult role, in this approach, is to be an active member of the group but in a supportive way. This could be by:

- encouraging the children to question each other and challenge each other's logic
- encouraging children to explain their thoughts
- allowing thinking time, free of pressure
- creating a safe environment in which pupils can take risks
- keeping the discussion focused on the question.

> **Reflection**
> Think about the similarities between the P4C approach and the features of a community of learners listed above.

Dialogic teaching: learning through talk

According to Alexander (2006) much more emphasis is placed on classroom talk in other European countries than is the case in British schools. He says, and I think most of us would agree, that in British schools 'considerably lower educational status is ascribed to talk than to writing, and this difference is constantly reinforced'. We are all used to asking pupils to write as evidence that they have learned and we all know pupils, and teachers, who think that classroom activities are not 'work' unless they involve producing a piece of writing. Alexander's research indicates that this difference in status between talking and writing is an aspect of an educational culture that is particularly British and he suggests that we should pay more attention to the place of talk in children's learning and development.

We know from Chapter 1 that the Vygotskian view of learning requires talk and interaction with others, adults and peers, because language, thinking and learning are very much related. Alexander builds on this important principle and suggests an approach to managing classroom talk for learning, which he calls 'dialogic teaching'. This approach requires certain conditions that clearly differentiate it from the familiar question and answer sessions found in many primary and secondary classrooms, where the teacher asks questions and the pupils give answers.

Principles of dialogic teaching

According to Alexander (2006: 26–7) dialogic teaching is:

- Collective: teachers and children address learning tasks together whether as a group or as a class, rather than in isolation.

- Reciprocal: teachers and pupils listen to each other, share ideas and consider alternative viewpoints.

- Supportive: children articulate their ideas freely, without fear of embarrassment over 'wrong' answers; and they help each other to reach common understandings.

- Cumulative: teachers and children build on their own and each others' ideas and chain them into coherent lines of thinking and enquiry.

- Purposeful: teachers plan and facilitate dialogic teaching with particular educational goals in view.

> **Reflection**
> Think about how dialogic teaching might support a community of learners.

Case study

During a CPD session a group of TAs engaged in the following 'jigsaw' task. 'Jigsawing' is a way of organizing group-work that requires collaboration and the putting together of information like the pieces of a jigsaw. In the first stage of the task small groups were given case studies from *Learning Without Limits* by Hart et al. (2004). Each case study described a teacher working with a class of pupils, some in primary schools and some in secondary. The group members were asked to read and discuss their chapter and then think about and record how a community of learning was being supported in the their classroom example. The second stage of the task required the formation of new groups made up of a member from each of the original groups. The new groups then shared their information and produced lists of features of a community of learning, using information from each group member. Below are some of the features identified during this activity.

Some features of a community of learning

- Social, emotional and intellectual activities are linked.
- The environment is safe – pupils feel they belong.
- Pupils understand the purpose of learning.
- The teacher is part of the team.
- Members of class show respect for each other.
- All contributions are valued.
- Lessons can be shaped by the pupils' contributions, so can be unpredictable.
- Pupils are in charge of their own learning.
- Everyone is included and given the opportunity to participate actively.
- Thinking time is built in.
- Pupils are grouped for performance rather than ability – no labels.
- The pupils learn from each other.
- Pupils are given choice.
- The teacher is interested in learning.
- There is a whole-school approach.
- The process of learning is more important than the finished piece of work.
- There is flexibility.
- Attention and respect is given to learning styles.
- Lessons are relevant and purposeful – well planned.
- Self-esteem and confidence are promoted.
- The teacher is a role model.

Teaching pupils to be learners: learning to learn

> Learning depends upon qualities of attention; of emotional reactivity; of thought and imagination; of reflection and self-awareness; and of sociability and relationships. (Claxton, 2004: 30)

So far in this chapter we have been discussing how groups of pupils and their teachers and support staff can work and learn together. We now need to spend some time thinking about how we can help our pupils to develop better attitudes to learning; how to help them to become better at learning. Government reports and documents and a body of educational research and discussion highlight the need for lifelong learning and the enhancement of basic skills.

> ... schools will need to devote attention to developing ... the dispositions of learners, and their learning skills, as well as developing formal instruction. (Estyn, 2003)

The idea of learning how to learn, as well as learning subject related content and skills, is now a very important part of school life in many schools and is seen to improve progress, as well as being a preparation for life.

Claxton (2004) discusses the term 'disposition', used by Estyn in the extract above. He says that learning involves the learner's 'attitudes, values, interests and beliefs' and that inappropriate teaching approaches can result in pupils becoming more 'able but less ready and willing'. To encourage our pupils to be 'ready' and 'willing' as well as 'able' we, as educators, need to help them to develop habits and tendencies, 'dispositions', that are useful to learners; habits such as persistence, asking questions and self-evaluation.

Four important learning habits, or dispositions, identified in Claxton (2002) and referred to by a number of other respected educational writers (for example, Lucas, 2002; Eaude, 2006; Wilmot, 2006) are the qualities of resilience, resourcefulness, reflectiveness and reciprocity. These are sometimes referred to as the 4Rs of learning. Let us examine each of these in turn and think about how they could be developed and promoted in the classroom.

Resilience

Resilience is about persevering or sticking at a task even though it may be difficult and there may be distractions. Life inside and outside school is full of distractions. Our pupils bring with them the effects, physical and emotional, of life at home and in the wider world, which often distract them from their learning. In school they are surrounded by the comings and goings that are part of life in a busy establishment involving large numbers of people and many different kinds of things. How can we help our pupils to cope with these internal and external distractions?

Eaude (2006) suggests that a calm, consistent and firm approach will provide a suitable environment for the development of resilience and that it is important for teachers and TAs to try to provide appropriate support: too much encourages the learner to become too dependent and too little may leave the learner feeling vulnerable. Claxton (2002) also talks about the need to help the learner manage distractions and points out that managing distractions is very much an individual matter. The calm and consistent environment, advocated by Eaude, will go some way towards helping some pupils and we, as educators, need to encourage our pupils to become aware of possible sources of distraction and how they can cope with them.

Maintaining concentration is another important aspect of resilience. In order for the learner to be inclined to concentrate it goes without saying that the activity in which we want them to engage must be relevant and meaningful. Of course, increased concentration is also developmental and comes with increasing maturity. Our expectations of perseverance and concentration must be realistic and tempered by our knowledge of the ages, stages and emotional needs of our pupils.

Question
How might you, as a TA, help your pupils to become more resilient learners?

Resourcefulness

A resourceful learner is one who is flexible in their approach to learning. He or she knows that there is more than one way of tackling a problem and is happy to learn with and from others in the class or group. Allowing children the freedom to make choices about some of things they learn, the resources they use and the method of communicating their learning will all help to develop resourcefulness in our pupils. The use of word banks and posters (see Chapter 3) will also encourage pupils to look beyond the adults in the classroom and to recognize themselves and each other as valuable resources.

We all recognize the pupil who comes across something in a book that they do not understand and immediately says 'I don't get it' and asks an adult. Wray and Lewis (1997) discuss the use of strategy charts to help pupils to try to solve problems before they ask for the teacher, or TA, for help. They describe the making of a chart to help pupils develop a strategy for overcoming difficulties in reading comprehension. They stress that the chart, or any classroom aid like this, is most effective when produced as a collaborative activity between pupils and teacher and a further requirement is that the adults in the classroom, teacher and TA, must remind pupils about the chart, refer pupils to it and put off any help until the pupil has used the chart.

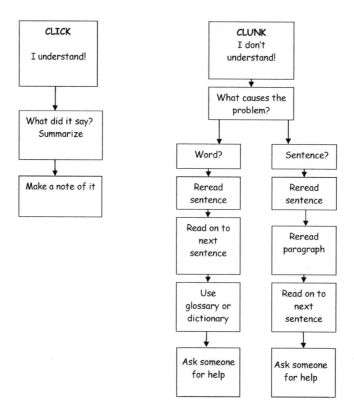

Figure 2: A chart to help pupils solve problems in reading comprehension (Wray and Lewis, 1997: 93)

Question
How might you, as a TA, help your pupils to become more resourceful learners?

Reflection

You will remember from Chapter 1 that social constructivist learning theory, using Vygotsky's ideas, places great emphasis on metacognition: awareness of and reflection on learning. Our classrooms and schools are very busy places. We feel that the curriculum is overcrowded and that there is not enough time to fit everything in. On top of that we are being encouraged to make our lessons challenging and 'pacey'. The consequence of this is that pupils are often not given the time to pause and reflect, or even to stop and think despite the fact that it is generally agreed that that good learning requires time for reflection and thought. We need to plan more for thinking time in our lessons, and we need to help our pupils to develop the habit of carefully thinking before answering questions, as we discussed in Chapter 4, and then reflecting on their learning. As Wilmot (2006: 13) says:

We don't always have to have hands-on learning, being constantly busy doing things; sometimes we need to make time for 'brains-on' learning, when we can do some deep thinking instead.

> **Question**
> How might you help your pupils to become more reflective learners?

Reciprocity

Social constructivist theory also emphasizes the importance of the social aspect of learning: learning with and from each other. Reciprocity means just this: being able to learn well with other people. Pupils need to develop a range of skills if we want them to work well together. They need to be able to take turns, to listen, to appreciate the points of view of others in the group and to accept and perhaps absorb the different ways of working and thinking shown by others. We discussed grouping for learning in Chapter 3 and noted the importance of arranging the size and membership of working groups according to the task and the learning rather than as a simple orga-nizational arrangement. Pupils need to have opportunities to work with friends but they also need opportunities to work with other pupils they would not necessarily choose to work with.

If we want our pupils to be able to work well in groups we must teach them how to do it and give them opportunities to practice. Drawing up a class set of rules for group-work will allow teacher and pupils to discuss how group members should behave towards each other and what group members should expect to contribute. Displaying the rules, referring to them, and reviewing and revising them from time to time will help to remind pupils until they become part of the classroom culture: 'the way we work in our classroom'.

> **Question**
> How might you help your pupils to become more reciprocating learners?

Responsibility

There is a fifth 'R', not mentioned in Claxton's 4Rs but referred to by other writers such as Wilmot (2006), and that is responsibility. Perhaps this 'disposition' is the basis of all the others because our pupils will not learn well unless they understand that they are responsible for their own learning. It is very difficult for adults in the classroom to stand back and not to 'chivvy' along our pupils when they are off-task. However, it is important that all pupils learn to be responsible and are able to accept the consequences if they do not work appropriately in class. A primary colleague, teacher of a Year 5 class, who works hard with her pupils to develop responsibility for learning, says that she constantly has to 'sit on her hands and bite her tongue' when pupils are off-task. She and her pupils work together to agree on the amount and quality of written work to be produced during a lesson. Pupils know that if work is not completed satisfactorily during the lesson they will have to complete it in their own time, at playtime or lunchtime and this system is accepted, with little fuss, by them all. They are learning, albeit painfully for some, that they need to accept responsibility for their own learning, and that they are also responsible, to some extent, for that of their friends.

Bringing it all together: reflection on the case study

The TAs in the case study above were working as a community of learners in their 'jigsaw' group activity. Can we apply Claxton's 4Rs to the TAs in their learning task?

The activity required each student to work in two different groups, thus practising social/reciprocating skills – as adults who had all worked together before there were no difficulties here. The group members offered each other support: they were able to help each other to work out any difficulties in understanding the texts being studied and they were able to agree upon methods of communicating their findings. They also persisted in the task and completed it. For a group of younger learners the task would have required both resourcefulness and resilience. The task was planned to allow sufficient thinking time and the discussion afterwards involved reflection on learning as well as on the content of the readings.

Case study

What follows is part of a learning log kept by a Year 5 pupil in a school that uses Claxton's 4Rs and makes time for the pupils to reflect on their learning. Each week time is set aside for the pupils to think about their learning during the week. They are given help, where needed, and encouraged to think about their learning in terms of one of the 4Rs.

Reflect on your learning recently This week we have been learning about writing a play script. We've been going around in different groups and trying out each other's scripts.	**Reflect on your learning recently** I have been learning about babies in RE. I didn't understand it at first but then listened more carefully and I got it.
Write about how you have been: <u>resilient</u>, resourceful, reflective, reciprocal. I have been resilient by getting so caught up in my work I forgot to go out to play.	**Write about how you have been: <u>resilient</u>, resourceful, reflective, reciprocal.** I have been resilient by noticing that one of my maths sums was wrong. So I put it right.
How might you be able to use what you have learned in the future? If I am a scriptwriter I would know some important things about writing a script.	**How might you be able to use what you have learned in the future?** If you're a teacher it will be good to know as much as you can.

Reflect on your learning recently I have learned this week to exaggerate in guided reading. Exaggerate is a little bit like fibbing but not naughty.	**Reflect on your learning recently** I have learned to improve my writing. It was hard when I had to change my handwriting.
Write about how you have been: resilient, resourceful, <u>reflective</u>, reciprocal. I was reflective when I thought back on a different way to work out a sum.	**Write about how you have been: resilient, <u>resourceful</u>, reflective, reciprocal.** I was resourceful when I got the dictionary out and looked up 'jumped'.
How might you be able to use what you have learned in the future? If you don't listen in at any subject and you have an exam coming you might fail.	**How might you be able to use what you have learned in the future?** Handwriting is going to be important if you have a job including writing and if they can't understand your writing it will be trouble.

This pupil still has a long way to go in her understanding of the concepts she is using but she is learning to use the language of reflection and she is developing the habit of thinking about her learning.

> **Reflection**
> Look back over this chapter and think about how working as a community of learners might help your pupils to learn how to learn.

Chapter summary

In this chapter we have been looking at two important sets of ideas to do with learning in the classroom: learning communities and learning to learn.

1. Learning communities involve shared relationships between adults in the classroom and pupils, and the understanding that all class members take the role of learner and leader of learning at different times.

2. Learning to learn is about the importance of developing positive attitudes to learning in order to learn well. These attitudes include:
   - resourcefulness
   - resilience
   - reflectiveness
   - reciprocity
   - responsibility.

6 Thinking for Learning

In this chapter we will be looking at thinking skills and thinking for learning. We will consider ideas about what is involved in thinking and the place of thinking within the curriculum, and then we will look at some ways in which you, as a TA, can play a part in developing your pupils' thinking skills. Before we start take a few minutes to reflect upon thinking. What do you think is involved? Are there different kinds of thinking? Can we be taught how to think?

What is thinking? How does it relate to learning?

> Thinking is involved in any mental activity that helps to formulate or solve a problem, to make a decision or to seek understanding. It is through thinking that we make meaning out of the world. (Fisher, 1990: 4)

You will notice that the above statement, made by someone who has been very influential in the area of 'teaching' thinking, does not attempt to define thinking but rather to identify it as a process. Many people, from the ancient Greeks to modern philosophers and educationists, have tried to understand the process so there are many points of view and there have been many attempts to describe and explain what happens when we think.

Piaget and Vygotsky, whom you met in Chapter 1, have both had a major influence on the development of teaching about thinking. Both believed that thinking was an active process and that intellectual development proceeded from active involvement with the world. Vygotsky's theory, that thought and language are fundamentally linked and that thinking and therefore learning is enhanced in a social context, has been particularly influential in the development of a number of 'thinking skills' programmes and curriculum strategies in England and Wales.

Do we need to teach our children to think?

> Although we are born with a capability to think, there is ample evidence that we can learn to think more effectively. (DCELLS, 2007: 10)

The more recent revisions of the National Curriculum and related national strategies and guidance documents place less emphasis on subject content and attach more importance to the development of a range of skills needed to be a successful learner and member of society. This is reflected in the discussion of curriculum futures in the current Primary Review:

> The curriculum of the future will need to focus on the evolving 'capabilities' needed by learners if they are to develop employability skills, live enriched lives and participate actively in democratic life. (Conroy, Hulme & Menter, 2008: 3)

The development of thinking has been identified as one of the 'key' or 'basic' skills for learning and life. *The Primary National Strategy* (DfES, 2004) in England refers to a range of 'key aspects of learning' which include creativity, information processing, reasoning, evaluation, enquiry and problem solving – all of which are included in the broad collection of 'thinking skills'. *The Primary Framework for Literacy and Mathematics* (DfES, 2006) gives guidance on embedding the key aspects of learning within literacy and numeracy and gives an overview of the expected progression in their development. The following examples from Foundation stage, Year 1 and Year 6 give a flavour of this progression in the skills related to thinking.

Foundation stage	<ul><li>think creatively and imaginatively</li><li>communicate with others as they investigate or solve problems.</li></ul>
Year 1	<ul><li>use reasoning and enquiry skills as they engage with the meaning of texts</li><li>use problem-solving approaches when decoding new words or deciding how to 'pay' and 'give change' in a role-play context</li><li>begin to develop evaluative skills as they listen to other children tell a story or explain how they built a shape</li><li>become more critical thinkers when asked to sort shapes or to decide whether a shape they have made meets the conditions that were set.</li></ul>

Year 6	• use texts as evidence, applying their own knowledge and experience to interpret and understand them
	• critically evaluate the usefulness of texts for specific purposes, bias and accuracy
	• evaluating other people's writing provides the criteria and tools to judge the effectiveness of their own writing
	• in mathematics, children discuss and compare alternative approaches to solving a problem
	• try different approaches and strategies when struggling to solve a problem or to explain a concept to others
	• modify steps towards a solution in the light of feedback
	• challenge their own and others' assumptions.

The Key Stage 3 National Strategy continues to highlight the importance of developing thinking skills, and the *Leading in Learning* programme (DfES, 2005b) has been developed to support teachers and schools in the teaching of thinking skills across the curriculum, in secondary schools.

> Leading in Learning ... involves the systematic and explicit development of thinking and learning skills and strategies across the curriculum. It enables pupils to understand themselves better as learners and to apply a widening repertoire of learning approaches in different subjects. Giving explicit attention to thinking and learning equips pupils to transfer their learning to different contexts and helps them to process, construct and deploy subject knowledge and understanding more actively and effectively. (DfES, 2005b: 5)

The revised curriculum in Wales, although set out differently from the English, also has an explicit emphasis on the development of skills, including thinking, across the curriculum. Here we see a particular definition of thinking, and the guidance documents for the revised curriculum focus upon particular aspects of the thinking process.

> Developing thinking can be defined as developing patterns of ideas that help learners acquire deeper understanding and enable them to explore and make sense of their world. It refers to processes of thinking that we have defined as plan, develop and reflect. (DCELLS, 2007: 10)

The Department for Children, Education and Lifelong Learning in Wales (DCELLS) has produced a non-statutory framework to guide the organization and progression in the development of thinking, communication, ICT and number skills for all children and young people from 3 to 19 years. The skills are then identified in individual subject documents to show how they can be developed across the curriculum and through the Key Stages, including post 16. Table 3 shows some examples of the expected progression in thinking skills, within personal and social education.

Table 3: Expected progression in thinking skills, within personal and social education

Foundation phase (3–7)	• children are encouraged to become independent thinkers and learners • children begin to develop an awareness of what they are good at and understand how they can improve their learning and use feedback to improve their work • children engage in activities that allow them to solve problems and discuss outcomes. (DCELLS, 2008a)
Key Stage 2	Learners should be given opportunities to: • distinguish between facts, beliefs and opinions • form personal opinions and make informed decisions.
Key Stage 3	Learners should be given opportunities to: • identify and assess bias and reliability • consider others' views to inform opinions and make informed decisions and choices.
Key Stage 4	Learners should be given opportunities to: • analyse information and ideas in order to assess bias, reliability and validity • take different perspectives into account when making informed decisions and choices. (DCELLS, 2008b)

What kinds of thinking are there?

The Primary Review, currently being conducted under the lead of Professor Robin Alexander, has reported on a wide range of aspects of primary education in England, including an examination of how current trends might develop in the future. Within this context they discuss some popular thinking skills programmes and they conclude that:

> A commitment to developing young children's capacity to think and reason is a core concern threaded through a range of approaches that emphasize critical and creative thinking and the development of personal autonomy. (Conroy, Hulme & Menter, 2008: 4)

Some curriculum documents and guidance materials tend to take a particular view of thinking and emphasize the importance of developing particular thinking skills in order to improve learning. The Welsh guidance, for instance, highlights the thinking processes involved in planning, developing and reflecting. However, there are views of thinking that go much wider than this and you may find that your school or educational setting is working with some of these. We will discuss just a small number of the many approaches to teaching thinking.

Activating children's thinking skills: Carol McGuinness

McGuinness (2000) (in McGregor, 2007: 21) suggests that thinking should be taught explicitly across the curriculum and that students should be helped to develop a thinking attitude or 'disposition'. You will notice that she uses the same terms here as Claxton in Chapter 5. She feels that there are six particular kinds of thinking that students need to develop in order to become effective learners:

1. Being able to identify and recognize patterns and relationships through processes such as classifying, comparing, sorting and making connections.

2. Being able to adopt a critical perspective: examine their own and other people's ideas critically.

3. Being creative and flexible, looking for alternatives and new ideas.

4. Solving problems.

5. Making decisions.

6. Being reflective and aware of their own thinking and learning – metacognition.

> **Reflection**
> Can you include any of these kinds of thinking in the work you do with your pupils? Which do you think are appropriate for Foundation stage children? Which for KS2? Are any particularly suited to older students? How might you encourage your pupils to develop a thinking 'disposition'?

Thinking for learning: Rockett and Percival

Rockett and Percival (2002) relate their view of thinking to some of the ideas we find in *Accelerated Learning*, see Smith (1998), Smith and Call (1999). Rockett and Percival (2002) identify an array of thinking skills that they feel are important for learners:

- sequencing and ordering information
- sorting and classifying and grouping
- analysing and identifying relationships
- comparing and contrasting
- making predictions, hypothesizing
- drawing conclusions
- recognizing bias and reliability
- brainstorming and generating ideas
- recognizing cause and effect and fair tests

- defining and clarifying problems
- thinking up solutions
- setting goals and sub-goals
- testing and evaluating outcomes
- planning and monitoring
- making decisions
- setting priorities
- identifying pros and cons.

As you can see the list of skills here is wide ranging; many are the same as Carol McGuinness's, and most of these can be approached and developed at any age or stage and in any setting. It should be possible to build them into learning activities across the curriculum and to help pupils to become aware of the processes by making explicit references to the skills being used so that they learn the language and are able to use it when talking about their own learning.

> **Reflection**
> Think about some of the work you have done in the past few days. Could you have made opportunities to work on one or more of the thinking skills in Rockett and Percival's list?

Six thinking hats: Edward de Bono

Edward de Bono has worked for many years to promote the teaching of thinking and has been very influential in developing approaches to the explicit teaching of thinking skills. One particular area of his work is of great relevance to problem solving, both in and outside the classroom situation. He suggests that in order to solve problems effectively we need to adopt a system of 'parallel' thinking which means thinking about a problem in a number of different ways, all of equal importance, in order to explore it fully. De Bono has identified six different ways or 'directions' of thinking in his 'six thinking hat' method (De Bono, 2000). He describes each kind of thinking in detail and awards each one a particular coloured hat, related to the kind of thinking, as an aid to memory.

Table 4: Six thinking hats – De Bono (2000)

Red hat	This kind of thinking concerns the emotions and is about how you feel about a situation – there is no need to justify or explain the feelings.
Yellow hat	This is positive, 'sunny' thinking; thinking about strengths, positive aspects, good points.
Black hat	As the colour suggests this is thinking about weaknesses and bad points but it is also about being careful, cautious, evaluating and making judgements.
Green hat	Green is the colour of growth and this kind of thinking is about new ideas and being creative.
White hat	This is thinking which is concerned with facts, figures, and information; it is objective and neutral.
Blue hat	Blue hat is about thinking about thinking and about the control and organization of solving the problem in question.

Jackson and Pickwell (2002: 36) give an interesting example of how the 'thinking hats' method can be applied to the study of a distant place in KS2 geography. Their study focuses on different aspects of life in India, both rural and urban, and they suggest using the hats as a basis for exploration and enquiry, using activities and questions such as those shown in Table 5.

Table 5: Application of thinking hats method

Red hat	Look at the photograph of traffic in the streets of Bangalore. How would you feel riding along in a rickshaw?
Yellow hat	How has farming changed over the years as a result of help from ActionAid?
Black hat	What might cause the rice crop to fail?
Green hat	Develop a dance based on the monsoon and the River Ganges.
White hat	Use the internet and reference books to create a data file on India.
Blue hat	What have we learned so far about India?

> **Reflection**
> Let us apply a little 'blue hat' thinking – what do you think about De Bono's six different ways of thinking? Do you think they could be useful in your classroom?

Philosophy for Children (P4C): Mathew Lipman

Mathew Lipman, an American professor of philosophy, developed the Philosophy for Children programme because, as a teacher, he was concerned that his students seemed unable to think clearly for themselves even though they were able to learn facts and give other people's opinions. Lipman wanted his students to become more thoughtful and reflective and he felt that the best way for them to develop a thoughtful and reflective disposition was by engaging in careful and cooperative dialogue within a community of enquiry (see Chapter 5). He felt strongly that it was important to start early, at the beginning of schooling, and that thinking should be taught explicitly but should also permeate the curriculum.

Many primary and some secondary schools use P4C regularly in a range of curriculum contexts and it is a particularly appropriate strategy for personal and social education and for addressing moral issues. There are training courses, both accredited and non-accredited, in P4C and in order for the approach to be of most benefit to pupils it is important that staff are trained. There are many schools where TAs are involved in 'Philosophy Club' or actively involved in communities of enquiry in the classroom.

Let us briefly look at part of an enquiry intended for KS2 personal and social education, using the story of *The Ugly Duckling* by Hans Christian Anderson. The example is taken from a teaching resource produced by CEWC CYMRU – full details in the 'Where Can You Go Next' section at the end of the book. Stories and pictures are often used as stimuli and pupils are invited to think and then raise questions, which are used to guide the discussion. The intention is that pupils generate their own questions but it can be useful to have some appropriately philosophical questions in case the pupils get stuck or run out of ideas. Having read and thought about the story of the *Ugly Duckling* some suggested questions for discussion are:

- Why didn't the mother duck take the older duck's advice and abandon the big egg?
- Is it ever right to judge someone by their appearance?
- Why do people make fun of each other?
- What does being 'ugly' or 'beautiful' mean?
- What did the mother mean when she said 'he is not so very ugly after all if you look at him properly'?

You can see that the questions are not the usual comprehension or story related questions; they address moral issues and concepts that underpin much of real life. The story is a vehicle that enables the issues and concepts to arise.

Concept mapping

Concept maps are useful devices that can be used at various times throughout a project. They are particularly useful at the beginning of a new topic because they can be used to raise pupils' prior knowledge and give an overview of the scope of a topic. They are also useful as an ongoing review and reflection tool, as pupils can add to them as they meet new ideas and acquire new information, and they can be used as an assessment tool at the end of a topic to revisit initial concepts and check understanding. Concept maps are useful tools for organizing and extending pupils' thinking because they encourage them to make connections between ideas and to express these connections in interesting ways: colours, pictures and symbols can all be used, as well as writing. With support this can lead to extended thinking and to the development of pupils' own questions to carry an enquiry forward.

There are several ways of going about organizing concept maps. They can be started with a brainstorm of what pupils know and think and these initial ideas can then be grouped and categorized. The categories and concepts resulting from this stage can then be used as a framework to develop extended and related concepts. Alternatively you can present the pupils with a set of concept cards, which they can discuss and organize, encouraging them to identify related ideas and make links between them.

Case study

A local primary school uses concept mapping throughout the school, from Early Years to Year 6. Junior pupils use them to help to plan new topics. The class teacher knows the content areas she needs to include to meet curriculum requirements but the pupils are invited to add to these and to contribute to the organization of the topic. They do this by constructing concept maps in which they link their ideas about the topic, what they think is interesting and what they would like to find out about, to curriculum subjects.

The school uses concept maps at the beginning of most, but not all topics, and the pupils have become used to referring to them as the topic progresses. In fact, individual pupils often choose to use them as an organizational tool during group and individual work. They are also used at the end of a topic to check up on some of things that have been learned.

How can you, as a TA, help to develop your pupils' thinking skills?

TAs work in many capacities in many different classroom situations. Some have a great deal of autonomy and some have little; some work in mainstream classrooms giving general support and some work with individuals or small groups of learners with special educational needs. Whatever the setting, it should be possible to work in a way that helps to develop thinking.

Questioning

Asking questions is something all classroom practitioners do but it is a part of our practice that it would be good to reflect upon. Good questions can help our pupils to think; they can help in the development of a thoughtful disposition. So how can we make sure that our questioning is 'thought provoking'? Wragg and Brown (2001: 28) suggest a list of 'errors' in questioning that make a useful checklist.

Common 'errors' in questioning
- Asking too many questions at once.
- Asking a question and answering it yourself.
- Asking questions only of the brightest or most likeable pupils.
- Asking a difficult question too early in the sequence of events.
- Asking irrelevant questions.
- Always asking the same type of questions (for example, closed ones).
- Asking questions in a threatening way.
- Not using probing questions.
- Not giving pupils time to think.
- Not correcting wrong answers.
- Ignoring pupils' answers.
- Failing to see the implications of pupils' answers.
- Failing to build on answers.

Some of these errors in questioning may not be relevant for you if you work primarily on a one to one basis but some will. Use the list to reflect on your work.

The Key Stage 3 National Strategy (DfES, 2003: 6) gives a useful list of the questioning skills that we, as educators, need to develop:

Common teaching skills: questioning
- Questions need to be planned in a sequence that guides pupils towards and reinforces the main objectives of the lesson.
- Certain types of question have inbuilt challenge and require pupils to think deeply:
  - open-ended questions that have no one obvious answer
  - questions that demand and develop higher-order thinking skills such as analysis, synthesis and evaluation
  - questions that encourage pupils to speculate and take risks.
- Teachers should build in 'wait time' so that pupils can reflect on a challenging question before answering it.
- Questions can be used to promote active listening and engagement, especially

when the 'no hands up' rule is used. Active listening skills can be developed further by building variety into a teacher's questions and expecting pupils to generate their own questions.
• Teachers can encourage pupils to give extended answers using questions and other strategies, such as inviting pupils to elaborate or speculate on a topic.

Some of these ideas reiterate those we have met in earlier chapters in the context of planning and assessment, and learning to learn. Whether you work in primary or secondary settings, or with individuals, groups or whole classes of pupils, questioning is an important skill to work on and develop in order to help your pupils to think.

Activities for one to one or small group-work

There are many activities that you can organize, for individuals or for small groups, which help to develop thinking, usually by stimulating discussion.

• Sequencing and matching activities are common practice in most primary and secondary class-rooms. They can be used in many curriculum areas and can involve combinations of artefacts, pictures or text.

• Sorting and classifying are widely used activities – you have seen an adult sorting activity in Chapter 2. Again, you can use artefacts, pictures and text and if the activity is done as a group the discussion, negotiation and decision making contribute to the quality of thinking, as would using a Venn diagram as a sorting device.

• Ranking activities are very useful, especially with older pupils. A ranking exercise differs from sequencing in that it requires judgement and the application of criteria. Items can be ranked as on a ladder or you can use a variation such as 'diamond ranking' where, as the name suggests, the items to be ranked are arranged in a diamond formation.

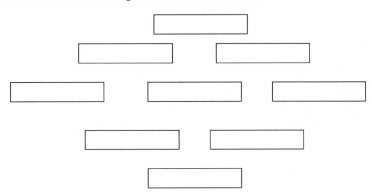

Figure 3: Diamond ranking

A task to try for yourself

The statements below are all qualities of a good group member. Rank them in a diamond formation according to how important you think they are, with the most important at the top, the two of next importance below, followed by the next three, then the next two, then the final statement.

The statements were written for adults and they come from Cottrell (2004) *The Study Skills Handbook*, but they could be adapted for use in the classroom. The focus of the exercise was working in groups and the point of the ranking exercise was to stimulate discussion and shared understanding, not to achieve the right answer because there isn't one.

Qualities of a good group member
- BE ENCOURAGING
For example, say 'I found that interesting'.
- SUM UP FOR THE GROUP
Well, we've agreed this so far ...
- LISTEN TO OTHER GROUP MEMBERS
Everyone deserves respectful attention.
- HELP THE FLOW
Contribute but don't dominate.
Ask reasonable questions.
Take some responsibility.
Help to keep to subject.
- BUILD ON OTHER PEOPLE'S IDEAS
- INCLUDE EVERYONE
Speak to everyone and make sure that everyone has chance to answer.
- INDICATE WHEN YOU AGREE
Express your agreement.
- ADMIT MISTAKES/MISUNDERSTANDINGS.
- OFFER INFORMATION
- USE BODY LANGUAGE
Smile, nod and so on.
- IF YOU DISAGREE
Don't simply reject, explore the idea.
- MAKE SUGGESTIONS

These are just a small number of easy to organize activities that pupils enjoy and that help to develop their thinking. There are many interesting resources available to support thinking skills; you probably have some in school.

Task
Look back at Rockett and Percival's list of thinking skills. Think about the group and individual activities suggested above and match them with the skills in the list. Try out an activity that is new to you with a small group of pupils and observe their response.

Reflection
Think about the links between Chapters 5 and 6. Try to express the main ideas in a concept map.

Chapter summary

In this chapter we have looked at some of the many views of thinking and considered the place of teaching thinking in the school curriculum. We have also considered some activities that should not be too difficult for TAs to organize in the context of one to one or group-work. Two important ideas for you to take away from this chapter could be:

1. Thinking can be taught and developed.
2. We all have a part to play in developing the quality of our pupils' thinking.

7 Supporting Learning for Pupils with Special Educational Needs

Chapter Outline

What do we mean by special educational needs?

Learning difficulties

Special learning difficulties (SLD)

More able, gifted and talented: a short note

Chapter summary and moving on

Glossary of terms relating to SEN and disabilities

This chapter looks at special educational needs (SEN) and the impact that those needs can have on the learning process – and therefore of course on the work you do as a TA. Although SEN is sometimes referred to as additional support needs, we will use the term SEN in this chapter, and provide a general outline of some of the implications of SEN in the classroom. This is a huge area. Our purpose here is to raise your awareness of some of the issues, provide you with information about other resources that are available if you wish to pursue the topic, and make suggestions for how you can more effectively support learning for pupils with SEN.

One of the most important things to remember is that as a TA you work under the direction of a teacher or other professional – perhaps a SENCO (special educational needs coordinator). This being the case your role is to provide designated support for the pupil, not to design programmes or interventions. Make sure you know exactly what is expected of you, and always ask if you are not sure. Some pupils have very particular needs and require very specific types of support. Check with your supervising teacher to make sure you understand your role and responsibilities.

Reflection

Before reading the rest of the chapter, stop a moment to ask yourself these questions:

- How would I define 'special educational needs'?
- What experiences have I had with pupils with special educational needs?
- What have those experiences taught me about pupils with SEN?

What do we mean by special educational needs?

According to the 1996 Education Act:

> A pupil has special educational needs if he or she has a learning difficulty which calls for special educational provision to be made for him or her.

However the Act also states that if a pupil has a 'disability, which prevents or hinders them from making use of education facilities', this also constitutes a learning difficulty, if it calls for special educational provision to be made. That means provision that is additional to or different from what is normally available to pupils of the same age. So in legal terms, 'learning difficulties' has a broader meaning than you might generally give it because it includes pupils who have a disability (such as hearing or visual impairment), which requires additional or different provision to be made for them, even if they have no cognitive difficulties or are not actually behind in their learning. In this chapter we will largely be considering the somewhat narrower meaning of learning difficulties, as provision for disabilities such as hearing or visual impairments are quite specialized, and you would need to consult directly with your local expert if you were assigned to work with a pupil with these types of disabilities.

In short pupils may have a special educational need if:

- Despite appropriate activities, planning and support they continue to experience a greater difficulty than their peers in learning and developing skills.
- They find it harder to learn than other pupils of the same age.
- They have a learning difficulty that calls for additional provision or some different teaching arrangements to be made for them.

Special educational needs can be the result of:

- physical impairment
- problems with vision, hearing, or speech
- developmental delay

- a medical condition
- social, communication, emotional or behavioural difficulties
- speech and language difficulties.

The 1970 Education Act ended the practice of excluding some pupils from school on the grounds that they were considered 'ineducable' because of disabilities. These were not just the sorts of pupils who would now attend special schools, but also thousands of pupils who had attended (or even lived in) special care units, training centres and hospitals. Since then we have become accustomed to pupils with a wide range of abilities in our schools, and now the principle of 'inclusive education' tries to ensure that pupils with SEN are educated together with their peers to the greatest possible extent. If you are interested in knowing more about how we got to where we now are in this respect, try the Inclusion UK website (http://inclusion.uwe.ac.uk).

The following details some of the more recent policy and legislation relating to SEN.

Legislation and policies supporting SEN in England and Wales

- **2001: Special Educational Needs and Disability Act (SENDA)**

  This Act amended the 1995 Disability Discrimination Act to make more explicit the need to anticipate as well as eradicate discrimination on the basis of SEN.

- **2001 Inclusive Schooling: Pupils with SEN**

  Statutory guidance giving practical advice on how to operate an inclusive school system.

- **2002 Revised SEN Code of Practice**

  Re-emphasized that the needs of pupils with SEN must be met, whenever possible in a mainstream setting; and that pupils and their parents should be consulted on the process.

- **2004 SEN and Disability: Towards Inclusive Schools**

  An Ofsted report reiterating the need to continue working towards inclusive practice.

- **2004 Removing Barriers to Achievement**

  The government's strategy for SEN establishing priorities for early intervention, raising expectations through developing teacher skills, and improving partnerships between schools and other services to meet family needs.

- **2004 Every Child Matters: Change for Children**

  Focuses on five outcomes for children: being healthy and safe, enjoying and achieving, making a positive contribution and achieving economic well-being.

- **2005 The Disability Discrimination Act (DDA)**

  This Act amends to 1995 DDA to include the legal duty of schools to promote equal opportunities for people with disabilities.

- **2006 Inclusion: Does it matter where pupils are taught?**

  An Ofsted report on factors that promote good outcomes for pupils with learning difficulties.

Special educational needs in mainstream schools

For most pupils with identified special educational needs, their needs can be met in a mainstream school. This may take the form of extra help (such as many of you provide as TAs), a different way of teaching the pupil, or special equipment. This is often referred to as 'school action' and is the simplest and most immediate solution to many pupils' difficulties. If the pupil doesn't make sufficient progress under these arrangements, other specialists can be brought in, for example an educational psychologist, or speech and language therapist, to provide additional advice and assessment. This stage of the process is often referred to as 'school action plus'. If these measures are not sufficient, the school (or the parents) can ask the LEA for a statutory assessment of special educational needs. If the results of the assessment, made by education specialists but also consulting parents, show that the pupil needs more help, the LEA must write a statement of special educational needs, which describes the pupil's needs and the ways in which those needs will be met. This happens for only about three per cent of pupils. Statements are reviewed annually, with teachers and parents invited to take part in review meetings. The pupil's statement should contain the following elements:

- A summary of the pupil's needs and strengths.
- A description of the additional support that will be provided by the school (for example, small group tutoring) or outside agencies (for example, weekly speech therapy).
- Targets for learning and, if appropriate, behaviour.

The statement should also detail whether the pupil will be disapplied from any aspects of the curriculum, for example, a pupil with speech and language difficulties may be disapplied from modern language classes in secondary school, in order to have additional speech/language therapy. The statement constitutes a legal agreement between the LEA and the parents. As a TA, if you work with a pupil with SEN who has a statement you may not have sight of that statement, but you should be aware of the targets the pupil is working to. The following terms relate to SEN and statements.

Terms relating to statements of SEN

- **Annual review**

  The review of a statement of special educational needs which an LEA must make within 12 months of making the statement or of the previous review.

- **Disapplication**

  Removal or lifting of a programme of study, attainment target, assessment, or any other component of the National Curriculum, including entire subjects or the entire National Curriculum.

- **Integration**

  Educating pupils with SEN together with pupils without SEN in mainstream schools wherever possible, and ensuring that pupils with SEN engage as much as possible in the activities of the school.

- **Modification**

  Amendment or alteration of a programme of study, attainment target, assessment or any other component of the National Curriculum, to give the pupil access to that area of the curriculum.

- **Named person**

  The person whom the LEA must identify when sending the parents a final version of a statement. The named person must be someone who can give the parents information and advice about their pupil's SEN. He or she can attend meetings with parents and encourage parental participation throughout the process. The named person should be independent of the LEA.

- **Note in lieu**

  A note issued to the pupil's parents and school when, following a statutory assessment, the LEA decide not to make a statement. The note should describe the pupil's SEN, explain why the LEA will not make a statement and make recommendations about appropriate provision for the pupil.

- **Responsible person**

  The headteacher or a school governor, who must be informed by the LEA when a pupil at a school has SEN. The responsible person must then ensure that all those who will teach the pupil know about his or her special educational needs.

- **SEN coordinator (SENCO)**

  Member of staff with responsibility for coordinating SEN provision in the school. In a small school the headteacher or deputy may take on this role.

- **SEN & Disability Tribunal (SENDIST)**

  An independent tribunal for determining appeals by parents against the LEA about pupils' special educational needs, if parents cannot reach agreement with the LEA. SENDIST also considers parents' claims of disability discrimination in schools.

- **Transition plan**

  This should form part of the first annual review after the pupil's fourteenth birthday, and all subsequent reviews. The purpose of the plan is to draw together information from a range of individuals in order to plan coherently for the young person's transition to adult life.

Task

The following table shows different disabilities or learning difficulties and the frequency with which they occur in school pupils. As you look at the table ask yourself these questions:
- Which of these special educational needs or disabilities are represented in the school where you work?
- Are you surprised by any of the figures shown in the table?

Table 6: Frequency of different types of SEN in schools in England (DfES, 2004)

TYPE OF NEED	PRIMARY	%	SECONDARY	%
Specific learning difficulty	41,780	14.5	41,250	19.6
Moderate learning difficulty	85,310	29.6	58,100	27.7
Severe learning difficulty	7,340	2.5	3,070	1.5
Profound and multiple learning difficulty	1,150	0.4	260	0.1
Behavioural, emotional and social difficulties	52,560	18.2	61,930	29.5
Speech, language and communications needs	50,130	17.4	10,720	5.1
Hearing impairment	6,090	2.1	5,130	2.4
Visual impairment	3,510	1.2	2,650	1.3
Multisensory impairment	510	0.2	180	0.1
Physical disability	11,790	4.1	7,540	3.6
Autistic spectrum disorder	15,950	5.5	6,710	3.2
Other difficulty/disability	12,180	4.2	12,370	5.9

Learning difficulties

The World Health Organization tells us that a learning disability is:

> a state of arrested or incomplete development of mind, with significant impairment of intellectual functioning and significant impairment of adaptive/social functioning.

This means that a pupil with learning difficulties may experience problems with:

- understanding
- learning or remembering something new
- generalizing what they have learned to a new situation.

They may then also have difficulties with:

- communication
- self-care
- awareness of health and safety.

In the UK learning difficulties are categorized as moderate, severe or profound. Although the technical definition of each of these categories has been based on IQ scores in the past, there is now much more emphasis on the level of support that people need to live independent lives. In relation to education, pupils with severe learning difficulties will almost always attend a special school and a small proportion of those pupils will have profound and multiple learning difficulties (PMLD) which means, as the name suggests, that they have several types of learning difficulty in combination.

A very important point to remember is that most of these difficulties will not go away, because they are caused by the way the pupil's mind functions, so pupils with learning difficulties grow up to be adults with learning difficulties. This may seem a very pessimistic view, but we mean it to be realistic. The good news is that, as with most difficulties, the severity is directly affected by context. A particular difficulty may be emphasized or minimized according to the place and activity the person finds themselves in. So if you think you are a poor runner, for example, that 'difficulty' or lack of ability would seem very acute if you tried racing against professional athletes. But running around playing with a toddler would be a different matter. You may be out of breath at the end but your lack of speed would not matter. As a TA you have direct influence over the classroom context when you work with pupils. There are many ways in which you can reduce the impact of their learning difficulties by adapting the environment and modifying the way you work.

Specific learning difficulties (SLD)

If we think of learning difficulties as being on a continuum or spectrum, at the least severe end are what are commonly known in the UK as specific learning difficulties (SLD). These include:

- dyslexia: particular difficulty with language
- dyscalculia: difficulties with numbers
- dyspraxia: immature or impaired development of movement (at its simplest, clumsiness).

These are problems within the pupil, in a sense, but solutions are available to us in school. As we have already stated, it is the interaction between the pupil's abilities and the school environment that can cause tensions and problems. You can make the difference by adjusting the environment to better suit the pupil. The suggestions we make here for pupils with SLD will be helpful for all pupils.

Pupils with SLD can experience difficulties in many areas of school life, some of which are listed in the following table.

Table 7: Areas of difficulty related to SLD

Organization	Speaking or writing	Memory
Knowing the time/date	Language	Following directions
Managing time	Learning/pronouncing words	Learning times tables
Completing tasks	Discriminating between	Learning new procedures
Finding belongings	sounds	Learning the alphabet
Putting things in order	Telling or writing stories	Identifying letters
Carrying out a plan	Understanding questions	Remembering names
Making decisions	Answering questions	Remembering events
Setting priorities	Following directions	Revising for tests
	Reading comprehension	
	Spelling	
Physical coordination	**Attention and concentration**	**Social behaviour**
Manipulating small objects	Completing a task	Making/keeping friends
Learning self-help skills	Acting before thinking	Impulsive behaviour
Cutting	Waiting	Low frustration tolerance
Drawing	Restlessness	Sportsmanship
Handwriting	Daydreaming	Accepting changes in routine
Climbing and running	Distractibility	Interpreting non-verbal clues
Mastering sports	Carrying out requests	(body language)
		Working cooperatively

Let us discuss some of these areas in more detail and look at ways in which you can help to minimize the effects.

Attention span

It is a common misconception that pupils with learning difficulties are unable to concentrate or pay attention. In fact they do pay attention, but to everything. They are easily distracted, because anything and everything can draw their attention. It is important to make the distinction between paying attention to nothing and paying attention to everything. The pupil's difficulty lies in being able to focus on one thing for a length of time and block everything else out. You may be one of the many TAs employed to keep a pupil like this on-task and focused on the learning activity.

What you can do:

1. Organize the seating arrangement so that distractions are minimized, for example not facing a friend or beside the door.

2. Break up the task into short parts, which can be tackled one at a time (a more refined version of what needs to happen for most of our pupils).

Processing language

Pupils with SLD have difficulty processing language, so when you ask a question other pupils will be processing an answer but the pupil with SLD will still be processing the question. Cognitively, this means they have double the workload. This difficulty in processing language also has an impact on reading and reading comprehension. Reading comprehension is often taught on the basis of teaching the meaning of the words, or ensuring that the pupil knows the vocabulary. We assume that if we explain all the 'big words' a pupil will be able to understand what they are reading. But reading comprehension is much more complex than that. We may know all of the words in a passage but not be able to make sense of it. We may even be able to answer questions about a passage, using the big words that we don't understand, but not have any real sense of what it all means. Reading comprehension presents real difficulties for pupils with SLD. To begin with, the reading task itself is likely to take up all of an individual's energy and cognitive space as they process the written language. This means that there is no capacity left for processing the content of the reading, or answering questions on the material. And, of course, as a pupil progresses through school more and more learning will depend upon an ability to process language, especially in written form.

What you can do:

1. Give pupils more processing time. Tell all of them that you're going to ask a question and give them time to think before you ask for an answer – then remember to wait before you allow anyone to answer. This should be a familiar technique as we have mentioned it in earlier chapters.

2. If you are asking for an answer with several components, for example 'Tell me three animals that live in the desert' or 'What were the two main causes of the First World War?' ask the pupil with SLD for the first answer. While the other pupils may have thought of three straight away, the pupil with SLD will probably only have thought of one. If you allow him or her to give that one answer then ask another pupil for one answer and so on, you can include more pupils in the process, including the one with SLD.

3. Don't repeat a question if the pupil doesn't answer immediately; you will interrupt their processing and may have to start all over again.

4. Make sure you offer information in both an auditory and visual format whenever possible. Offer books on tape, read a passage out loud instead of just having the pupil read it silently, and read through any written instructions out loud, rather than assuming the pupil will understand what is required. The multisensory input is particularly important for a pupil with SLD.

Visual perception

It is often the case that we may be able to see something but not necessarily perceive its meaning. Think of the pictures made up of dots of colour, which were very popular some years ago. Are you one of those people who could stand and admire the picture? Or are you the one who looks at it and says, 'That's just dots. I can't see a picture!' You feel as if you are the only one who can't see it, when in reality many people can only see the dots (some won't want to admit to it). A pupil with SLD is often the only one in the class who can't 'see' what everyone else can, and that adds to the problem. They may want to see but motivation only allows us to do something we are capable of. Pupils with SLD cannot be bribed or persuaded to see or perceive meaning.

What you can do:

1. In situations where it is obvious that the pupil cannot understand what is being explained, or cannot 'see' a point that is being made, be patient and provide guidance and teaching. Show the pupil and explain, and then move on, returning to the problem later if necessary.

Visual-motor (hand-eye) coordination

Pupils with SLD often have difficulties in translating what they see into the necessary action. They receive mixed messages from their eyes (visual) and hands (motor) systems and have trouble integrating the messages. Writing, and particularly copying from the board or from a book, can therefore be particularly difficult for them. Under these circumstances, writing is a cognitive task and it takes a great deal of concentration. There is no way that they can listen and take notes because they have to devote all of their energy to writing and have no cognitive space left for listening or thinking.

> **Task and reflection**
> Find a simple line drawing (something from a pupil's colouring book, for example) and place it on the table in front of you, then stand a small mirror up on the table at the top of your page of drawing. Now trace around the outlines of the drawing, but don't look at the page itself – look in the mirror as you draw.
>
> Suddenly your mind will be telling you to go one way and your instinct, and hand, will be going the other way. These are the sorts of mixed messages that pupils with SLD can get.
>
> How did you feel as you were doing this? What was your resulting drawing like?

One of the typical results is very slow and untidy work, especially handwriting. Although there may be some small benefits in pupils copying from a book or the board, more of it will not make the pupil with SLD any faster or better at it.

What you can do:

1. One of your assigned roles may be to take notes, perhaps for a student in secondary school. Even if you have not been assigned to do this, wherever possible try to get or make a copy of any work the student needs to do beforehand, so that he or she can start in on the work straight away rather than having to spend time and energy on the copying part of the task. Help your student to get straight to the important task of processing the information rather than just copying it.

2. Use talk as a learning tool. It is increasingly being recognized that talk facilitates thinking and learning, as you will remember from earlier chapters. As a TA if you are assigned to an individual student or a small group, make use of talk and discussion to help students process information and develop their thinking. This in turn will facilitate written language production.

Oral expression

Pupils with SLD often speak in a very disjointed and confused way. This is part of their processing difficulty. Many of them have a word-finding problem (dysnomia), so they go all round the houses trying to say something quite simple. In simple terms the brain consists of two systems: storage and retrieval. Pupils with SLD have trouble both retrieving information and storing it in a place where they can find it again. Another factor to consider is the distinction between what are sometimes called associative tasks and cognitive tasks. You can only do one cognitive task at a time, because it takes up all your attention or cognitive space; you can do more than one associative task at a time, because associative tasks do not require all of your attention. For pupils with SLD speaking is a cognitive rather than an associative task.

Take driving, for instance. Most of the time you can talk or think (even eat) while you are driving: what we call being on automatic pilot. But as soon as someone steps out in front of the car, or you hit road works or bad road conditions, your mind switches from auto pilot to paying careful attention: driving has moved from being associative to being cognitive. You can no longer chat as easily with your passengers and you may turn the radio down. These are instinctive reactions to the need to pay attention to the now cognitive task of driving.

What you can do:

1. Only ask the pupil to do one thing at a time, and don't interrupt them when they are in the middle of a task. They will not be able to chat while working, for example, or dig into their bag for their homework, without interrupting the task in hand.

2. Give instructions one at a time. We often issue strings of instructions, for example *'Put your books away in your drawer and then sit back down at your tables. You only need a pencil and ruler for the next thing we're doing.'* Look at how many components there are in that sentence! The pupil with SLD may set off towards his drawer but by the time he gets there he won't remember what he was supposed to do, and he's very unlikely to end up back at his table with the relevant equipment. He's much more likely to stop and chat to his friends.

Risk-taking

Pupils with learning difficulties quickly learn not to take risks. Sometimes this is because there is little or no reward for being right, but mostly because they are so often wrong and there is little incentive to risk getting involved or responding to a question. Lack of willingness to take risks in the classroom can lead to withdrawal from active participation in lessons, and what may look like stubbornness or defiance. Another interpretation might be avoidance, because a natural human reaction to anxiety is to look away.

What you can do:

1. Don't insist that a pupil looks at you or makes eye contact when you are working with them. It is less intimidating if they are allowed to look away, particularly if they are unsure and anxious.

2. Make sure you acknowledge and reward effort and correct responses (for all pupils) and use incorrect answers as instructional opportunities. No pupil should feel punished for giving a wrong answer. You ask questions partly to determine what pupils have learned. If they can't give you the right answer that is a signal to you that you need to go back over the material.

Above all:

- Don't use sarcasm. It may be the only thing that stays with the pupil from your interactions with him or her that day, because it affects their self-esteem. As you know, children and adults are more able to learn when they feel good about themselves.

- Recognize that anxiety seriously affects performance and make allowances for the pupil with SLD when they are in more stressful situations, for example reading aloud in class, or dealing with an unexpected situation.

- Don't use rhetorical questions, for example, 'How many times do I have to tell you not to do that?' There is no good answer the pupil can give, and that is belittling.

- Be aware that school is not only a source of tension and anxiety for a pupil with SLD, but can also be exhausting. The constant need to concentrate and give careful attention to academic tasks, as well as social interactions, can be physically very draining.

More able, gifted and talented: a short note

It may seem strange to include a section on able, gifted and talented pupils in a chapter on special educational needs. However, although most of these pupils may not have learning difficulties they will have some special educational needs.

> **Question**
> What does more able, gifted and talented mean? Are you familiar with these terms? Think about them and jot your ideas down. You may also want to ask your colleagues about their understanding of the terms.

Gifted, more able and talented pupils can be defined as pupils who have abilities, or potential abilities, beyond that of most of their peer group. Consequently they require a more challenging curriculum. In trying to understand the issues for these children it is useful to know what is generally meant by the terms we use:

- more able – ability in social and leadership areas
- gifted – academic ability
- talented – ability in arts and physical areas.

What are the characteristics of these pupils?

The Department for Children, Schools and Families (DCSF) and the Qualification and Curriculum Council (QCA) have each highlighted general characteristics including:

- Being a good reader.
- Being very articulate or verbally fluent for their age.
- Giving quick verbal responses (which can appear cheeky).
- Having a wide general knowledge.
- Thinking quickly and accurately – having an ability to work things out in their head very quickly.

- Learning quickly.
- Being interested in topics that one might associate with an older child.
- Being determined, diligent and interested in uncovering patterns.
- Communicating well with adults – often better than with their peer group.
- Having a range of interests, some of which are almost obsessions.
- Showing unusual and original responses to problem-solving activities – generating creative working solutions.
- Preferring verbal to written activities.
- Being logical.
- Working systematically.
- Working flexibly, processing unfamiliar information and applying knowledge, experience and insight to unfamiliar situations.
- Being self-taught in their own interest areas.
- Having a good memory that they can access easily.
- Being artistic.
- Being musical.
- Excelling at sport.
- Demonstrating particular physical dexterity or skill.
- Having strong views and opinions.
- Making sound judgements.
- Having a lively and original imagination/sense of humour.
- Being very sensitive and aware.
- Focusing on their own interests rather than what is being taught.
- Being socially adept.
- Appearing arrogant or socially inept.
- Being easily bored by what they perceive as routine tasks.
- Showing a strong sense of leadership.
- Not necessarily being well behaved or well liked by others.

It is important to remember, however, that more able, gifted and talented children do not necessarily fit these expectations. Not all of these pupils are obvious achievers; many actually underachieve and their potential can be hidden by factors such as low self-esteem, lack of challenge, frustration or even learning disabilities.

Identifying more able, gifted and talented pupils

Think about the characteristics described above. Now think about the children you work with. Do any of them exhibit any of these characteristics? Your role as a TA often allows you to develop a deep understanding of the children in your care; you see and things that the class teacher may not. *You are a key person in terms of identifying children who are more able, gifted and talented.*

Effective learning culture for more able, gifted and talented

So how can we develop an effective learning culture for more able, gifted and talented children? The potential they have to develop expertise can be tapped into through educational opportunities within the curriculum (and we mustn't forget extra-curricular activities) that provide:

- breadth – **enrichment**
- depth – **extension**
- pace – **acceleration.**

We can, and should, promote an atmosphere of inclusiveness where we challenge any negative stereotyped generalizations about gifted, more able and talented pupils.

If you are interested in finding out more about these pupils there are some suggestions in the 'Where Can You Go Next?' section at the end of the book.

Chapter summary and moving on

This chapter has given you general background information about special educational needs in mainstream schools. It has identified some of the problems that pupils with specific learning difficulties (SLD) might have and it has suggested some ways in which you, as a TA, can help the pupils with SLD that you work with. It has also noted that pupils who are able, gifted and talented need to be included as having special educational needs. You will have noticed that many of the ideas you have met in earlier chapters, in the context of supporting learning in general, are mentioned here again in the context of SEN.

To take you further we have a glossary of terms relating to SEN and disabilities that you might encounter in school and there are references to support materials and websites in the 'Where Can You Go Next?' section of the book.

Glossary of terms relating to SEN and disabilities

Autistic Spectrum Disorder (ASD)

Autistic spectrum disorder is a relatively new term that recognizes that there are a number of sub-groups within the spectrum of autism. Pupils with autistic spectrum disorder find it difficult to:

- understand and use non-verbal and verbal communication
- understand social behaviour – which affects their ability to interact with pupils and adults
- think and behave flexibly – which may be shown in restricted, obsessional or repetitive activities.

Pupils with ASD cover the full range of ability and the severity of their impairment varies widely. Some pupils also have learning disabilities or other difficulties, making diagnosis difficult.

Pupils with autistic spectrum disorders may have a difficulty in understanding the communication of others and in developing effective communication themselves. Many are delayed in learning to speak and some never develop meaningful speech.

Pupils find it difficult to understand the social behaviour of others. They are literal thinkers and fail to understand the social context. They can experience high levels of stress and anxiety in settings that don't meet their needs or when routines are changed. This can lead to inappropriate behaviour.

Some pupils with ASD have a different perception of sounds, sights, smell, touch and taste and this affects their response to these sensations. They may have unusual sleep and behaviour patterns.

Young pupils may not play with toys in a conventional and imaginative way but instead use toys rigidly or repetitively, for example watching moving parts of machinery for long periods with intense concentration. They have difficulty adapting to new situations and often prefer routine.

Pupils with Asperger's syndrome should be recorded in this category. These pupils share the same triad of impairments but have higher intellectual abilities and their language development is different from the majority of pupils with autism.

Dyscalculia

Pupils with dyscalculia have difficulty in acquiring mathematical skills. Pupils may have difficulty understanding simple number concepts, lack an intuitive grasp of numbers and have problems learning number facts and procedures.

Dyslexia

Pupils with dyslexia have a marked and persistent difficulty in learning to read, write and spell, despite progress in other areas. Pupils may have poor reading comprehension, handwriting and punctuation. They may also have difficulties in concentration and organization and in remembering sequences of words. They may mispronounce common words or reverse letters and sounds in words.

Dyspraxia

Pupils with dyspraxia are affected by an impairment or immaturity of the organization of movement, often appearing clumsy. Gross and fine motor skills are hard to learn and difficult to retain and generalize. Pupils may have poor balance and coordination and may be hesitant in many actions (running, skipping, hopping, holding a pencil, doing jigsaws, and so on). Their articulation may also be immature and their language late to develop. They may also have poor awareness of body position and poor social skills.

Hearing impairment (HI)

Pupils with a hearing impairment range from those with a mild hearing loss to those who are profoundly deaf. For educational purposes, they are regarded as having a hearing impairment if they require hearing aids, adaptations to their environment and/or particular teaching strategies in order to access the concepts and language of the curriculum. A number of pupils with a hearing impairment also have an additional disability or learning difficulty. Hearing loss may be because of conductive or sensori-neural problems and can be measured on a decibel scale. Four categories are generally used: mild, moderate, severe and profound. Some pupils with a significant loss communicate through sign instead of, or as well as, speech.

Moderate learning difficulty (MLD)

Pupils with moderate learning difficulties will have attainments significantly below expected levels in most areas of the curriculum, despite appropriate interventions. Their needs will not be able to be met by normal differentiation and the flexibilities of the National Curriculum. They should only be recorded as MLD if additional educational provision is being made to help them to access the curriculum. Pupils with moderate learning difficulties have much greater difficulty than their peers in acquiring basic literacy and numeracy skills and in understanding concepts. They may also have associated speech and language delay, low self-esteem, low levels of concentration and under-developed social skills.

Multisensory impairment (MSI)

Pupils with multisensory impairment have a combination of visual and hearing difficulties. They are sometimes referred to as deafblind but may have residual sight and/or hearing. Many also have additional disabilities but their complex needs mean that it may be difficult to ascertain their intellectual abilities. Pupils with multisensory impairment have much greater difficulties in accessing the curriculum and the environment than those with a single sensory impairment. They have difficulties in perception, communication and in the acquisition of information. Incidental learning is limited. The combination can result in high anxiety and multisensory deprivation. Pupils need teaching approaches that make good use of their residual hearing and vision, together with their other senses. They may need alternative means of communication.

Physical disability (PD)

There is a wide range of physical disabilities and pupils cover the whole ability range. Some pupils are able to access the curriculum and learn effectively without additional educational provision. They have a disability but do not have a special educational need. For others, the impact on their education may be severe. A medical diagnosis does not necessarily mean that a pupil has SEN. It depends on the impact the condition has on their educational needs. There are several medical conditions associated with physical disability that can impact on mobility. These include cerebral palsy, heart disease, spina bifida and hydrocephalus, and muscular dystrophy. Pupils with physical disabilities may also have sensory impairments, neurological problems or learning difficulties. Some pupils are mobile but have significant fine motor difficulties that require support. Others may need augmentative or alternative communication aids.

Profound and multiple learning difficulty (PMLD)

Pupils with PMLD have complex learning needs. In addition to very severe learning difficulties, they have other significant difficulties, such as physical disabilities, sensory impairment or a severe medical condition. Pupils require a high level of adult support, both for their learning needs and also for their personal care. They are likely to need sensory stimulation and a curriculum broken down into very small steps. Some pupils communicate by gesture, eye pointing or symbols, others by very simple language. Their attainments are likely to remain below level 1 of the National Curriculum throughout their school careers.

Severe learning difficulty (SLD)

Pupils with severe learning difficulties have significant intellectual or cognitive impairments. This has a major effect on their ability to participate in the school curriculum without support. They may also have difficulties in mobility and coordination, communication and perception and the acquisition of self-help skills. Pupils with severe learning difficulties will need support in all areas of the curriculum. They may also require teaching of self-help, independence and social skills. Some pupils may use sign and symbols but most will be able to hold simple conversations. Their attainments may be below level 1 of the National Curriculum for much of their school careers.

8 Where Can You Go Next?

There are many sources of information that will help you in your work as a TA. Learning Support magazine, available from www.learningsupport.co.uk is a useful publication and the English and Welsh government and curriculum sites hold a wide range of information and support materials. All the curriculum documents and guidance materials can be downloaded from these sites.

- www.dfes.gov.uk – this is the website for the Department for Children, Families and Schools (the former DfES)
- www.new.wales.gov.uk – the website for the Department for Children, Education, Lifelong Learning and Skills (the former DELLS)
- www.standards.dfes.gov.uk
- www.teachernet.gov.uk
- www.qca.org.uk

A small selection of books and other resources is listed below, arranged under chapter headings.

What is learning? How does it happen?

Overall, L. (2007) *Supporting Children's Learning: A Guide for Teaching Assistants*, London: Sage
Pound, L. and Hughes, K. (2005) *How Children Learn: From Montessori to Vygotsky – Educational Theories and Approaches Made Easy*, Step Forward Publishing Ltd
Pritchard, A. (2005) *Ways of Learning – Learning Theories and Learning Styles in the Classroom*, London: David Fulton

Learning styles and multiple intelligences

There are so many books and other publications that deal with learning styles and with the social and emotional aspects of learning that it will not be difficult for you to find further information. A good place to start would be with the DfES website and a look at *Excellence and Enjoyment: the Social and Emotional Aspects of Learning* – the full reference is in the reference list.

The learning environment

There are many basic classroom management books, aimed at student teachers that would help you to move on. For example:

Arthur, J., Grainger, T. and Wray, D. (2006) *Learning to Teach in the Primary School*, London: Routledgefalmer
Capel, S., Leask, M. and Turner, T. (2005) *Learning to Teach in the Secondary School: A Companion to School Experience*, Taylor & Francis
Hayes, D. (2001) *Foundations of Primary Teaching (2nd Edition)*, London: David Fulton

The learning cycle: planning and assessment

There is a great deal of information and support on the websites at the beginning of this section.

Shirley Clarke has written a number of useful and very readable books on the subject of assessment for learning. She has a website to which you can refer for details of all her books: www.shirleyclarke-education.org. Two of her most recent books are:

Clarke, S. (2005) *Formative Assessment in the Secondary Classroom*, London: Hodder & Stoughton
Clarke, S. (2005) *Formative Assessment in Action – Weaving the Elements Together*, London: Hodder Education

Learning to learn and thinking for learning

I have put these sections together because there is considerable overlap in support materials. The standards website is a good place to start: www.standards.dfes.gov.uk/thinkingskills/ and then there is the website for Philosophy for Children:

www.sapere.org.uk. Network Press produces resources for P4C, including for infants: www.networkpress.co.uk

A useful and easy publication to use is:

CEWC CYMRU (2005) *Thinking Citizens: How to Make PSE Philosophical*, Cardiff: Council for Education in World Citizenship-Cymru

It is produced by the Council for Education in World Citizenship-Cymru and available from: www.cewc-cymru.org.uk

'Inspiration' and 'Kidspiration', software for mind mapping, suitable for use in schools is available from www.taglearning.com

Supporting learning for pupils with special educational needs

Information on special educational needs is readily available. Use the National Association for Special Educational Needs (NASEN) – www.nasen.org.uk and the Institute of Learning Difficulties (BILD) – www.bild.org.uk
   There are books about SEN written for TAs, for example:

Birkett, V. and Barnes, R. (2003) *How to Support and Teach Children with Special Educational Needs*, LDA
Cartwright, A. and Morgan, J. (2008) *A Teaching Assistants' Guide to Autistic Spectrum Disorders*, London: Continuum
Reid, G. and Green, S. (2007) *A Teaching Assistants' Guide to Dyslexia*, London: Continuum

For information about more able, gifted and talented pupils try the QCA website and the Standards website, as above, and also the National Literacy Trust website: www.literacytrust.org.uk. The National Academy for Gifted and Talented Youth website (NAGTY): www.warwick.ac.uk/gifted might be useful.
   For further reading try:

Mclachlan, A. (2002) *Raising the Standard: Addressing the Needs of Gifted and*

Talented Pupils, London: Centre for Information on Language Teaching and Research

Smith, C.M.M. (2005) *Teaching Gifted and Talented Pupils in the Primary School: a Practical Guide*, London: Paul Chapman

Teare, J.B. (1997) *Effective Provision for Able and Talented Children*, Stafford: Network Educational Press

References

Alexander, R. (2006) *Towards Dialogic Teaching*, UK: Dialogos

Becta (2005) *Learning Styles – an introduction to the research literature*. Available at: http://industry.becta.org.uk/display.cfm?resID=15472

Black, P., Harrison, C., Lee, C., Marshall, B., Wiliam, D. (2002) *Working Inside the Black Box: Assessment for Learning in the Classroom*, London: School of Education, King's College

Black, P., Harrison, C., Lee, C., Marshall, B., Wiliam, D. (2003) *Assessment for Learning: Putting it into Practice*, Maidenhead: Oxford University Press

Cardiff Advisory Service for Education (2004) *Learning to Learn. Enquiries into Building Resourceful, Resilient and Reflective Learners*, Cardiff: City and County of Cardiff

Clarke, S. (1998) *Targeting Assessment in the Primary Classroom*, London: Hodder & Stoughton

Clarke, S. (2001) *Unlocking Formative Assessment*, London: Hodder & Stoughton

Clarke, S. (2003) *Enriching Feedback*, London: Hodder & Stoughton

Clarke, S. (2005) *Formative Assessment in Action – Weaving the Elements Together*, London: Hodder Education

Claxton, G. (2002) *Building Learning Power*, Bristol: TLO

Claxton, G. (2004) *Teaching Children to Learn*, Birmingham: National Primary Trust

Claxton, G. (2005) *An Intelligent Look at Emotional Intelligence*, London: ATL

Conroy, J., Hulme, M., and Menter, I. (2008) *Primary Curriculum Futures, Primary Review Research Survey 3/3*, Cambridge: The Primary Review. Available at: www.primaryreview.org.uk

Cottrell, S. (2004) *The Study Skills Handbook*, Basingstoke: Palgrave Macmillan

Davenport, C. (1996) *An Introduction to Child Development*, London: Collins

Dean, J. (2001) *Organising Learning in the Primary School (3rd Edition)*, London: RoutledgeFalmer

DeBono, E. (2000) *Six Thinking Hats*, London: Penguin

DCELLS (2007) *Skills Framework for 3 to 19-Year-Olds in Wales*, Cardiff: Welsh Assembly Government

DCELLS (2008a) *Framework for Children's Learning for 3 to 17-Year-Olds in Wales*, Cardiff: Welsh Assembly Government

DCELLS (2008b) *Personal and Social Education Framework for 7 to 19-Year-Olds in Wales*, Cardiff: Welsh Assembly Government

DfES (2003) *Key Stage 3 National Strategy Key Messages: Pedagogy and Practice*, London: HMSO

DfES (2004) *Statistics of Schools in England*, Norwich: HMSO

DfES (2004) *Excellence and Enjoyment, Learning and Teaching in the Primary Years*, London: HMSO

DfES (2005a) *Excellence and Enjoyment: the Social and Emotional Aspects of Learning*, London: HMSO

DfES (2005b) *Key Stage 3 National Strategy. Leading in Learning: Developing Thinking Skills at Key Stage 3, Guide for School Leaders*, London: HMSO

DfES (2006) *National Primary Strategy: Primary Framework for Literacy and Mathematics*, London: HMSO

Dixon, A. (2004) 'Selfhood's Playground', *Times Educational Supplement*, 13 August 2004

Donaldson, M. (1981) *Children's Minds*, London: Collins

Eaude, T. (2006) *Children's Spiritual, Moral, Social and Cultural Development*, Exeter: Learning Matters

Estyn (2003) *Excellent Schools: A Vision for Schools in Wales in the 21st Century*, Cardiff: HMSO

Fisher, R. (1990) *Teaching Children to Think*, Cheltenham: Stanley Thornes

Gardner, H. (1983) *Frames of Mind: The Theory of Multiple Intelligences*, New York: Basic Books

Ginnis, P. (2002) *The Teacher's Toolkit*, Carmarthen: Crown House

Goleman, D. (1996) *Emotional Intelligence. Why It Can Matter More than IQ*, London: Bloomsbury

Hart, S., Dixon A., Drummond, M.J., McIntyre, D., (2004) *Learning Without Limits*, Maidenhead: Open University Press

Hayes, D. (2001) *Foundations of Primary Teaching (2nd Edition)*, London: David Fulton

Hughes, M. (1999) *Closing the Learning Gap*, Stafford: Network Educational Press

Ikin, J., Ratcliff, R., Drake, J. (2000) *Teaching Skills: A Toolbox For Improvement*, Birmingham: National Primary Trust

Jackson, E. and Pickwell, L. (2002) 'Put On Your Thinking Hats', *Primary Geographer*, April 2002

Laar, B., Blatchford, R., Winkley, D., Badman, G., Howard, R., (1996) *Effective Teaching*, Oxford: National Primary Centre

Lucas, B. (2002) *Power Up Your Mind*, London: Nicholas Brierley

McGregor, D. (2007) *Developing Thinking Developing Learning*, Maidenhead: Open University Press

McGuinness, C. (2000) 'Caught in the ACTS', *Teaching Thinking*, 1(2), 48–52, in McGregor (2007)

Palmer, S. and Dolya, G. (2004) 'Freedom of Thought', *Times Educational Supplement*, 30 July 2004

Rockett, M. and Percival, S. (2002) *Thinking for Learning*, Stafford: Network Educational Press

Sage, R. and Wilkie, M. (2003) *Supporting Learning in Primary Schools*, Exeter: Learning Matters

Smith, A. (1998) *Accelerated Learning in the Classroom*, Stafford: Network Educational Press Ltd

Smith, A. and Call, N. (1999) *The Alps Approach: Accelerated Learning in Primary Schools*, Stafford: Network Educational Press Ltd

Watkins, C. (2001) *Learning about Learning Enhances Performance*, London: Institute of Education School Improvement Network (Research Matters series No 13)

Watkins, C. (2003) *Learning: a Sense-maker's Guide*, London: ATL

Weare, K. (2004) *Developing the Emotionally Literate School*, London: Paul Chapman

Wilmot, E. (2006) *Personalising Learning in the Primary Classroom*, Carmarthen: Crown House Publishing

Wragg, E.C. and Brown, G. (2001) *Questioning in the Primary School*, London: RoutledgeFalmer

Wragg, E.C. (2004) 'An Icon of the Mind', *Times Educational Supplement*, 6 August 2004

Wray, D. and Lewis, M. (1997) *Extending Literacy. Children reading and Writing Non-Fiction*, London: Routledge

Index